The late-afternoon sun lights the smile lighting the face of five-year-old Gretchen-Kelly Tucker, sitting on the porch of her grandfather's house in Cherry Hill Park, Paget.

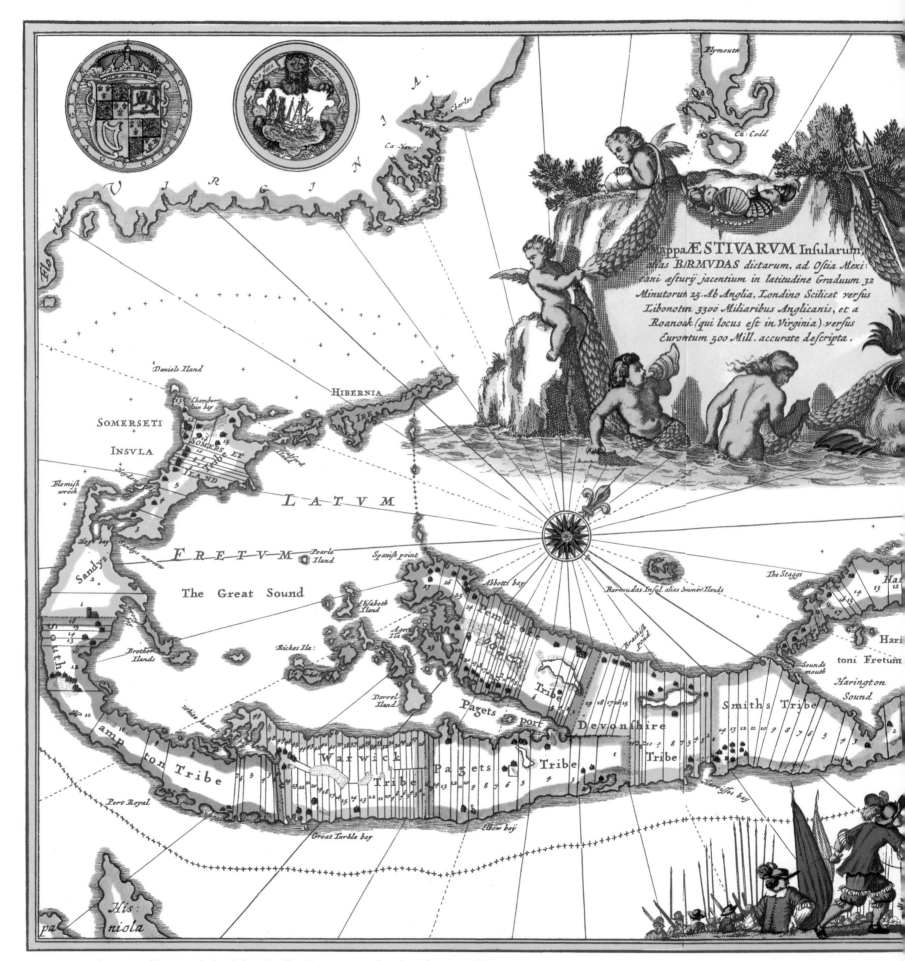

An early map of Bermuda by John Ogilby, Esq., printed in London in 1670.

For the people of Bermuda,
with admiration and affection
for the world they have
created and preserved

A late-summer sunrise seen from Astwood Park in Warwick Parish. East of the park, the coastline plunges to the surf below in a steep cliff, creating one of the most dramatic vistas in all of Bermuda.

Bermuda
A World Apart

Text and photographs by
Roger A. LaBrucherie

Imágenes Press

One of Bermuda's delights is the architectural beauty found in some of even her most humble buildings, such as this ivy-covered garage gracing Middle Road near Ely's Harbour in Sandys Parish.

Table of Contents

Foreword

Since I have now been photographing and writing about Bermuda as a photojournalist for well over fifteen years, it would be foolish of me to deny that I have developed a love affair with these remarkable islands. Indeed, the fact that I began the research and photography for my first book on Bermuda nearly two decades ago is a source of repeated astonishment for me, a constant reminder of the tendency of time to fly ever faster. Perhaps equally astonishing to me is the belief I once held that that first book, *Images of Bermuda*, contained all I had to convey about this enchanted world. But time, repeated visits to the island over the years, and my evolution as a photojournalist combined to disprove that notion.

As is true with most things in life, books begin to show their age after a time, and for the past three or four years I had been wanting to do an update of *Images of Bermuda*, and made several visits to the island to conduct research and take new photographs for such a revision. Each time I was about to begin the revising process, however, another project intervened, and the Bermuda project was delayed. Thus, by the time I was finally ready to go forward with the update, I had gathered so much new material that an entirely new book seemed appropriate.

Those familiar with my earlier work on Bermuda will see that this book shares the highly personal and impressionistic approach to the selection of photographs which characterized *Images of Bermuda*, but I have also attempted to give this new book a logical framework which will convey a great deal of information about the island and its history. In order to do so, I have included a considerable amount of archival art and photographs, as well as some new artwork especially commissioned to depict specific aspects of Bermuda's past.

Hopefully the result fulfills the ambition that I have always held for my books: that they be more than just collections of pretty pictures, and that they educate as well as entertain. It is for this reason that I call my works documentary books, and I have always hoped that they might serve as bridges to understanding in a world in which people of differing cultures and backgrounds increasingly come into contact with one another.

One result of my extended and repeated encounters with Bermuda and her people over the past fifteen years has been my growing realization that, the better I have come to know Bermuda, the more complex I realize her culture and society to be. While I harbor no illusions that I will ever fully understand this singular island and her people, neither, after such a warm and lengthy acquaintance, can I conceive of the day when Bermuda will no longer be a part of my life. God willing, I will have the pleasure of getting to know this remarkable world better for many years to come.

The south shore of the island is lined with a series of superb beaches, including Horseshoe Bay in Southampton Parish, the most popular of all among the island's visitors.

A Singular World

A sculpted "eyebrow" decorates the doorway of an old farm building in Paget.

An aerial view looking east toward Ely's Harbour reveals the shallow reefs which surround Bermuda and extend far to the north and west of the island. The reefs have played a vital protective role in Bermuda's history: throughout time, against the ravages of wave erosion, and later, after the settlement of the island, in providing a natural defense against sea-borne attack by England's enemies.

Tucker's Town Bay

Callan Glen, near Bailey's Bay in Hamilton Parish, is one of the most striking houses along Bermuda's north shore. The house dates from the early 1800s, and takes its name from its first owner and builder, Claude McCallan, one of the island's foremost nine-teenth-century shipwrights. A Scotsman, McCallan settled in Bermuda after being shipwrecked on the island's north reef.

A late-afternoon ferry crosses the sun-sparkled waters of Hamilton Harbour [above]. The harbour lies at the heart of the island, and ferries have been plying the harbour's waters for over two centuries. (William Zuill's *Bermuda Journey* notes that a sail-powered ferry was operating between Salt Kettle, on the Paget shore, and St. George's as early as 1794.)

More recent arrivals on the harbour scene, cruise ships moored at the Hamilton docks add sparkle of their own to a summer evening [facing page].

For a photojournalist, the coverage of a country's culture and people is as important as
its scenery, and a people's attitude to being photographed can say much about a national "personality." The man in the photograph above is Stanley Ray, sexton of the Bermuda
Cathedral, who posed for me in the doorway of the Cathedral's chapel in the spring of
1993. I had photographed the young schoolgirl on the facing page during a visit to her
primary-one classroom at the St. George's Preparatory School some years earlier. Both
portraits, I think, capture the openness and self-confidence of the Bermudian people,
and these characteristics make photographing people in Bermuda a sheer delight.

Founded in 1612, St. George's was the island's only town until the founding of Hamilton in the 1790s, and became a treasure trove of the colony's oldest buildings, including the Old State House, Bermuda's first stone building, dating from the early 1620s; the Globe Hotel, across from St. Peter's Church, from about 1699; the Old Rectory, about 1705; and the Tucker House, on Water Street, about 1711.

The Tucker's Town peninsula, seen here in an aerial view looking northeast, is home to some of the finest luxury houses in Bermuda. The name for the area, which is not in fact a town, originated in the early 1600s, with Governor Daniel Tucker's plan—never fulfilled—to place the colony's capital here, overlooking Castle Harbour. On the horizon lies St. David's Island, home to Bermuda's airport.

After serving for a century and a half as a key strategic outpost for the Royal Navy, the Dockyard at Bermuda's western tip was abandoned in the 1950s as Britain retrenched in the period after World War II. The loss of the military payroll and the Dockyard's civilian employment were severe economic blows, but the closing of the Dockyard presented an opportunity as well, and a program of conversion to civilian use began in the 1970s. Today the harbour provides docking facilities for visiting cruise ships, and the massive stone buildings which once served the Royal Navy now house commercial and tourist-related businesses and light industry, as well as the Bermuda Maritime Museum. The Clocktower Building, the most striking of the Dockyard structures [shown in interior and exterior views on these pages], has been transformed into an elegant shopping mall containing shops, galleries, and restaurants.

A springtime fixture for well over a century and a half, the Annual Agricultural Exhibition fills the Botanical Gardens each April with a wide variety of attractions and entertainments, including livestock and crafts exhibits, vegetable carving, and equestrian events [these pages]. Bermuda's equivalent of a county fair, the three-day "Ag Show" dates from 1840, when Governor William Reid organized the first such event, part of his continuing efforts to stimulate Bermudi-ans' interest in working the soil.

The sun rises over the Atlantic through the Natural Arches, on the beach at Tucker's Town near the Mid-Ocean Golf Course [this page]. Although the arches stood as an island attraction for centuries, strong hurricanes during the summer of 1995 severely eroded the beach beneath them. With the arches in imminent danger of collapse, work was begun to reinforce them in September of that year, not long after this photograph was taken.

Pitts Bay [facing page], opening on to Hamilton Harbour just west of the Hamilton Princess Hotel, provides a quiet anchorage near the capital.

The island's fleet of fitted dinghies race across Granaway Deep, part of a summer-long series to determine an annual champion. A class unique to Bermuda, the famed four-teen-foot craft evolved from the working sailboats which once plied Bermuda's waters.

A glorious "Bermudaful day" crowns the Southampton Princess Golf Course. Bermuda is a golfer's paradise, with eight eighteen-hole golf courses (and a ninth on the way), reputedly the highest concentration of courses per square mile in the world.

Chaplin Bay, one of a series of secluded beaches on the south shore in
Warwick and Southampton Parishes.

An aerial view from over Southampton Parish, looking eastward. In the center foreground stands Gibbs Hill Lighthouse; beyond the lighthouse and to the right is the Southampton Princess Hotel; beyond it to the left, at the edge of the Great Sound, is Riddell's Bay Golf Course. Beyond both stretch Warwick and Paget Parishes, with the City of Hamilton and Harrington Sound just visible in the distance.

The south shore east of Warwick's Astwood Park [facing page]. When the wind and waves are very strong, gusts of sea spray can drench the vantage point from which this photograph was taken, as I discovered one morning after a hurricane had passed near the island.

During the summer months, the longtail [above], is a common sight over the south shore, darting in and out of its cliffside nests. Also known as the tropicbird, the longtail has become a popular emblem of Bermuda, and its annual return to the island after a winter absence is taken as a first sign of spring's arrival.

No one has done more to defend and preserve natural Bermuda than Government Conservation Officer David Wingate, seen here walking with his dog Max on Nonsuch Island [above]. While still a teenager, he happened upon Spittal Pond in Smith's Parish [facing page], Bermuda's largest bird sanctuary, and gradually developed a passionate concern for Bermuda's environment.

When in 1951 the cahow, long thought extinct, was rediscovered nesting on some small islands in Castle Harbour, Dr. Wingate committed himself to a life's work of ensuring the bird's survival, moving to Nonsuch to build and safeguard nesting sites. Over the past four decades he has worked to recreate Nonsuch as a living museum of pre-colonial Bermuda, replacing imported exotic plants with native species. And the cahow? Although the bird's future is by no means secure, there is reason for cautious optimism: Nonsuch now counts about fifty breeding pairs—more than double the low point to which they had fallen in 1960.

A World Is Born

For a very, very long time—for time beyond measure—there was nothing. Nothing but the wind and the waves.

For aeons, the dark waves rolled and the wild winds swept over that deep, nameless sea. Then, in the midst of those aeons, and far below the floor of the sea itself, fiery red lava from deep within the earth found a fissure in the earth's crust and began surging upward. As it breached the sea floor and came in contact with cold seawater, the surface of the molten flow cooled and hardened. But so hot was the lava at its core that the flow continued its upward surge, and layer upon layer of fresh lava spread over and built upon lava that had hardened before.

And so, little by little, a mountain began to grow on the bottom of the sea. It would grow for a very long time, this underwater volcano, for here the sea was nearly three miles deep, and the volcano was unpredictable, at times adding to its bulk for years, at other times lying dormant for long intervals. And then one day, there came the crack and sizzle of fiery hot lava meeting air and water together, as the mountain at long last thrust above the surface of the sea. And in that moment, the island that would come to be known as Bermuda was born.

For uncounted millennia to come, the volcano would continue building the island, high above the sea and some twenty times larger than the island we know today. Just how high the island rose, no one can say for sure, but it was certainly several times higher than present-day Bermuda. And then, thirty to fifty million years ago, the volcano at last became dormant, as the heat deep beneath the mountain subsided and the core of the volcano slowly cooled and solidified.

But from the moment the mountain had risen above the sea, the forces of nature—this time in the form of the waves of the ocean and the rain carried on the wind—began the process of tearing it down. The aeons passed, and those inexorable natural forces eroded the island down to sea level and below, creating the 200-square-mile sea mount which underlies modern Bermuda and her surrounding reefs.

As the volcano gradually disappeared beneath the waves, ocean currents and waves now carried billions upon billions of sand-sized particles—the ground-up skeletons of marine life—to the island's beaches. From the beaches, these skeletal remains, composed of calcium carbonate, were lifted and carried across the island by the wind, creating aeolian (the word means wind-blown) dunes. Across hundreds of thousands of years and four ice ages, the island grew smaller and larger as the sea level rose and fell, at times extending the full width of the sea mount, while the wind built the hills so characteristic of the island's topography. Over time, rainwater seeping through the dunes cemented the particles into the sandy limestone rock, between two and four hundred feet thick, which caps Bermuda's volcanic base. To the north and west of the island, where the limestone cap lies underwater, calcareous algae and coral polyps have built extensive reefs over the remainder of the sea mount.

Thus, over an immense amount of time, the island was sculpted, as wind and waves carved bays, inlets, sounds, and headlands. Rain and atmospheric dust combined with the native limestone to begin building a thin soil, and currents of wind and sea, with the help of birds, brought the seeds of grasses, bushes, and trees, which took root in the island's thin soil, and in turn helped to build that soil. But the lush garden that is Bermuda today is deceptive, for plants and animals must overcome enormous odds to reach an island as remote as Bermuda, and today the vast bulk of the island's vegetation, including almost all of her flowering plants, has been introduced by man.

Despite the immense odds, the seeds of some plants did manage to reach the island's shores: among them were Spanish bayonet, prickly pear cactus, and mangrove, bay grape, wild olive, and palmetto trees, as well as Bermudiana, which produces the island's tiny namesake flower. Most prominent of all was the Bermuda cedar, actually a species of juniper, which practically carpeted the islands. (In the case of the last three mentioned, the plants evolved on the island into species unique, or *endemic,* to Bermuda.)

Even rarer was the flightless land animal that somehow reached the island—indeed, insects aside, only two, a land crab and a rock lizard known as a skink, managed to make that incredible journey and successfully reproduce. But the island's lack of land animals was compensated to a considerable extent by the creatures which traveled by air or sea and for whom Bermuda became home: fish, of course, and sea turtles, as well as bats and a great variety of sea birds which nested in the cliffs. Especially noteworthy was a species of petrel, known as the cahow (named for the sound of its call), which nested on the island in huge numbers and evolved into an endemic species. Periodically, birds migrating between the northern latitudes and the tropics were added to the resident fauna when they stopped on the island to rest and feed in the spring and fall.

Discovery

As the world reached the mid-point of the second millennium, A.D., Bermuda belonged to a select group: it remained one of the few habitable places on earth which man had not yet discovered and

A September dawn silhouettes the limestone headlands of the south shore near Sinky Bay [facing page]. A thin layer crowning an extinct volcano which rises nearly three miles from the sea floor, Bermuda's aeolian limestone is composed of the skeletal remains of tiny sea creatures. Ground into sand-sized particles by wave action, over aeons the tiny grains were then shaped by the wind and cemented by rain into Bermuda's characteristic hills.

The passage of time is visible in the hanging stalactites and the stalagmites of Crystal Cave [above], near Harrington Sound, as well. And the cave's stalagmites—submerged in a salt water pond which connects with the ocean—are evidence of yet another prehistoric phenomenon: for they were formed during the ice ages, when the world's sea level was far below today's level.

Marley Beach, a gorgeous
stretch of sand on the south
shore in Warwick, looks much
as it must have in aeons past.

settled. Geography alone is probably a sufficient expla-
nation, for volcanic accident had made Bermuda one of
the most isolated islands in the world. But coupled with
the island's isolation was the culture of the Indian peoples who inhabited the areas nearest to Bermuda, which
made them unlikely to fill the role of discoverers.

The North American continent, some six hundred
miles to the west (and Bermuda's closest landfall), had
been inhabited for perhaps twenty thousand years by
Asian peoples who had crossed the land bridge between
Siberia and Alaska during the Ice Age. But the tribes of
North America, blessed with an immensity of land and
without a seagoing tradition, had never had the need
nor desire to risk venturing into the open ocean.

Some eight hundred miles to the south, the islands of
the Caribbean had been home to Amerindian peoples
from before the time of Christ. Obviously, these tribes
had developed the ability to sail the open ocean. But the
stepping-stone pattern of the Caribbean island arc,
where most islands are within sight of another, meant
that the peoples of the Caribbean never had need to de-
velop long-distance ocean navigation skills (which the
Polynesians, for example, had used to explore and pop-

As is true of all islands, Bermuda was home to relatively few native species of flora and fauna, and (insects aside) only two land-based, flightless animals: the land crab and a rock lizard, or skink. Once common throughout Bermuda, the skink is now rarely seen, but thrives on the islands of Castle Harbour, including Nonsuch, where the one above was photographed.

When man first reached Bermuda it was covered in dense forest, and apart from the Bermuda cedar, no tree was more useful than the palmetto [facing page]. Its leaves were used for thatching the settlers' earliest buildings; its heart and berries were a food source for man and beast; and its sap was fermented into a potent liquor called bibby.

ulate the islands of the vast Pacific). And so when Bermuda was discovered, her discoverers came not from the west, nor from the south, but from the east, and the discoverers were Europeans.

The mariners of Europe had a seafaring tradition stretching back for centuries, but they had historically limited their sailing to the safety of coastal waters. By the early fifteenth century, however, technological advances in shipbuilding and navigation were making it possible for European ships to reliably sail out of sight of land and return to home port safely. In the vanguard of these efforts were the Portuguese, probing deep into the Atlantic under the leadership of their legendary prince, Henry the Navigator. By 1427 they had discovered the Azores, nearly a thousand miles to the west. But the real prize lay to the east—and over the next sixty years the Portuguese patiently worked their way down the coast of Africa, searching for the southern tip of the continent. Finally, in 1486, they rounded the Cape of Good Hope, sailed into the open water of the Indian Ocean, and were on their way to the silks and spices of the Indies. Domination of this lucrative ocean route to the Orient would make Portugal one of the richest and most powerful nations of 16th-century Europe.

The prospect of a Portuguese ascendancy was cause for great alarm among the Spanish, Portugal's long-time rivals. So when a Genoese sailor and map maker named Christopher Columbus came to King Ferdinand and Queen Isabella with his daring plan to reach the riches of the Indies by sailing westward, around the earth, he found an attentive audience. Unfortunately for Columbus, the king and queen were then enmeshed in a great struggle to oust the Moors from Spain, and he had to wait seven agonizing years before they agreed to sponsor his expedition. Finally, in the summer of 1492, his three little ships were ready, and on the third of August of that year Columbus left the port of Palos and sailed west toward his destiny—and the dawn of the New World.

Columbus's extraordinary voyage and subsequent discoveries and colonizations in and around the Caribbean Sea led to an Iberian domination of the New World which was to last for more than a century; by the early 1500s the routes to and from the new colonies had become a veritable Spanish highway. (Columbus's 1493 voyage to the West Indies—the second of the four he eventually made—counted seventeen ships and some 1500 colonists.) Thus it is hardly surprising that a Spanish sea captain, Juan de Bermúdez, is credited with discovering and giving name to Bermuda.

However, precisely *when* Bermúdez made his discovery is less certain. As one of the island's earliest historians, Major-General John Henry Lefroy, "Sometime Governor of the Bermudas," put it in his 1876 classic, *Memorials of the Bermudas*:

> *The discovery of the Bermudas followed very closely on that of the continent of America; exactly when and by whom the islands were first sighted is, however, a question involved in some obscurity.*

There is no dispute about when the first *documented* sighting of the island occurred: this visit was recorded for posterity by Spain's official historian, Gonzales Ferdinando d'Oviedo, when he and Bermúdez anchored their ship *La Garza* off the island in 1515. (Contrary winds prevented their landing, and Oviedo wrote a description of the island from some distance offshore.)

But over the years various researchers have noted that Oviedo's paragraph reporting *La Garza's* encounter with the island does not describe it as a *discovery,* and have argued that this omission implies that Bermúdez had actually discovered the island on a previous voyage. The late Terry Tucker, one of Bermuda's most prolific modern historians, maintained that 1503 was the probable discovery date. But her argument for that date rests on a very slender reed: a single French map, published *circa* 1690, which notes 1503 as the date of discovery. Other historians have come down in favor of 1505, when Bermúdez is known to have made a return voyage from Hispaniola to Spain. And finally, there is the map of Peter Martyr, published in 1511, which shows an island of uncertain shape and position north of the Bahamas, marked "la bermuda."

As Lefroy noted in 1876, there is considerable evidence suggesting that Bermuda was in fact discovered before 1515. But, *exactly when* before 1515 was, he concluded, a question "involved in some obscurity." It remains no less so today.

Isla de Demonios

While the precise year of Bermuda's discovery is likely to remain lost in the mists of the past, there is no doubt that the island soon became well known indeed to the mariners of the era, though not necessarily by the name Bermuda. After Ponce de León's discovery of the Gulf Stream in 1513, ships returning to Europe from the Caribbean began riding its current northeast to about latitude 33° North, where they turned east to run before the prevailing winds across the Atlantic.

There was one problem with this new route however: east of the Gulf Stream, at 32° North latitude, lay a small, low-rising island with extensive reefs stretching to the north and west. Given the imprecise navigational instruments of the day, those deadly reefs could bring grief to even the most cautious sea captains. Before long Bermuda's deadly reefs had claimed their first victims, and the island soon acquired a new name among Spanish sailors, a name which even found its way onto 16th-century maps: *La Isla de Demonios* (The Isle of Devils).

The number of ships and men lost to Bermuda's reefs will never be known with certainty, but two wrecks of the 16th century were well documented: in 1543 a Portuguese ship returning home from Santo Domingo ran aground on the reef north of the island, and the survivors spent two months ashore building a boat, which they succeeded in sailing back to Hispaniola. During their sojourn on the island, one of those castaways, it is believed, carved a rock with an inscription bearing that date and uncertain initials—the sole physical evidence of man's 16th-century presence on the island which would survive into the 20th century. (That rock, near Spittal Pond, would come to be known as Spanish Rock.)

Half a century later, a French ship struck the reef near North Rock, and the survivors were stranded on the island for five months. This wreck has gained a place in history because one of the castaways was an English sailor named Henry May, who upon his return to England in 1594 provided the first extensive English-language description of Bermuda.

Although Spain dominated the colonization of the New World throughout the sixteenth century, by the time Henry May's Bermuda narrative was being read it was obvious that Spain could no longer maintain a colonial monopoly in North America. Even as early as the 1520s, the Portuguese, French, and English had probed the northern reaches of North America for a sea-passage to the Orient. Stretched to the limit of her resources by the enormity of her colonial territory in the Caribbean, Mexico, Florida, and Central and South America, Spain had been powerless to prevent these incursions.

As the 1500s wore on, it gradually became apparent to the Europeans that this new continent was a vast territory which might be worth possessing in and of itself. By the latter part of the century,

Columbus's discovery of the New World in 1492 soon created a burgeoning ship traffic between the West Indies and Europe. Homeward-bound ships often passed between Florida and the Bahamas, riding the Gulf Stream northeast to about latitude 33° North, where they turned eastward before the prevailing winds. Their only obstacle, at 32° North latitude, was a tiny island encircled by a large reef. In the early 1500s, a Spanish sea captain, Juan Bermúdez, made the first documented sighting of that island, and it eventually took his name. But by the middle of the 16th century, sailors were calling Bermuda "The Isle of Devils"—for many a ship had come to grief on Bermuda's deadly reefs.

One shipwreck survivor—very probably the victim of a Portuguese vessel known to have run aground in 1543—carved that date, a cross, and uncertain initials high on a cliff overlooking the south shore near Spittal Pond. (Those carvings, which came to be known as Spanish Rock, were for centuries the oldest sign of man's presence on Bermuda. After time and the elements had nearly obliterated the original stone carving, it was replaced several decades ago by the bronze tablet replica seen on the facing page.) More than six decades after that unknown Portuguese left his mark, Bermuda's reefs would claim yet another victim, a westward-bound English ship, and that shipwreck would be the most momentous of Bermuda's history.

Storm-tossed and leaking badly, her inverted ensign signalling her distress, the Virginia-bound *Sea Venture* was at the point of sinking when Bermuda's reef caught the ship and held her fast. All aboard were safely ferried ashore, and over the next ten months the castaways would build two ships and then sail on to Jamestown. But two men remained behind, and so that fateful July 28, 1609, the date that spelled the end for the *Sea Venture*, also marks Bermuda's beginning as an English settlement.

both the English (on Roanoke Island, in present-day North Carolina) and the French (in South Carolina and Florida) had established short-lived colonies. Then, in 1588, came England's stunning defeat of the Invincible Armada. With this dramatic demonstration of the decline of Spanish sea power, the English, French, and Dutch began to colonize North America in earnest.

Disaster and Deliverance

In 1607, the Virginia Company of London established a new colony on Chesapeake Bay in Virginia, naming it Jamestown in honor of King James I. Two years later, in June of 1609, a relief fleet (consisting of seven ships and two smaller vessels called pinnaces) under the command of Admiral Sir George Somers set out from Plymouth, England, with additional settlers and supplies for the infant colony. Sir George commanded the fleet from his flagship, the 300-ton *Sea Venture*, which carried about 150 passengers and crew, among them Sir Thomas

Gates, the new governor of the Virginia colony.

After seven uneventful weeks at sea, the ships were struck by a severe storm which separated the fleet; a short time later, the Atlantic sailor's worst nightmare, a hurricane, hit the *Sea Venture*. Mountainous seas and terrifying winds racked the ship, but there was worse: the ship's seams began to open, and water poured into the hold. For four days and nights every man, woman, and child aboard pumped and bailed to exhaustion. Despite their herculean efforts, ten feet of water filled the bottom of the ship, and all appeared lost. And then, Sir George, at the helm, sighted land on the western horizon and ordered enough sail unfurled to drive toward the island. Half a mile from shore, the *Sea Venture* wedged in the reef, which held her fast as the storm blew itself out. As the waters calmed, the longboat was lowered and all aboard the *Sea Venture*, including the ship's dog, were ferried ashore onto what was later named St. George's Island.

The date was July 28, 1609, and although the Isle of Devils had claimed another ship, the joyous survivors no doubt saw the island of their salvation as closer to heaven than to hell. Unquestionably, the castaways had reason to think of Bermuda as an earthly paradise: the climate was agreeable, there were no hostile Indians, and there was food aplenty, in the form of fish, sea turtles, prickly pear, palmetto heart, berries, and wild olives. Most abundant of all were the eerily tame cahows, and the wild hogs which passing Spanish ships had loosed on the islands in the previous century as a precautionary food source for future shipwrecked sailors.

Indeed, among the castaways were those—Sir George Somers included, some have argued—who would have been happy to claim the island for England and found a new colony right there. But whatever some may have thought, the expedition's leaders knew their duty, and that was to press on to Jamestown. At Buildings Bay on St. George's Island, near where they had come ashore, the castaways began building a small ship, the *Deliverance*, using timbers and rigging salvaged from the *Sea Venture*. Since the *Deliverance* would be too small to carry all the survivors on to Virginia, Sir George Somers built a second, smaller vessel, a pinnace named *Patience*, entirely out of Bermuda cedar.

On May 10, 1610, nearly ten months after their fortuitous arrival, the survivors hoisted sail for Jamestown. Left behind on the island, apparently deserters, were Robert Waters and Christopher Carter, both of whom had been involved in mutinies in favor of remaining on the island, rather than continuing on to Virginia. (The reason Waters and Carter remained behind can never be known with certainty, although some have argued that they were involved in an intrigue with Somers, in which the Admiral planned to return to the island to establish a permanent colony. Whatever the reason, the fact that the two men did remain has marked July 28, 1609, as the date when Bermuda's continuous settlement began.)

After only two weeks' sail *Deliverance* and *Patience* reached Virginia. But the condition of the Jamestown colony surely made many of the *Sea Venture* castaways wish that they had sided with the rebels who had wanted to remain on Bermuda. For Jamestown was a scene of desolation: of some five hundred settlers who had come to the colony over the past three years, fewer than a hundred remained. Scores had died of starvation or disease, while others had been killed by hostile Indians. (Among the Jamestown settlers were those who had arrived on the other ships of the *Sea Venture* fleet, which had survived the hurricane and reached Virginia the year before.)

With starvation a continuing threat to the Jamestown settlers, Sir George volunteered to return to Bermuda to get hogs, fish, and other foodstuffs for the colony, and on June 19th he sailed for the island with a small party in the *Patience.* On arriving back in Bermuda, Somers and his crew found the two deserters, Waters and Carter, alive and well, and everyone set about the task of gathering food for Jamestown. But the previous eighteen months of sea voyages, shipwreck, and rough living had taken a fatal toll on Sir George, and on November 9, 1610, at the age of fifty-six, the hero of the *Sea Venture* died on the island which would thereafter bear his name.

After Sir George's death, his nephew, Matthew Somers, took charge, and decided to sail on to England, rather than return to Jamestown's aid. Once again, Waters and Carter would remain behind (this time indisputably by choice) along with a third man, Edward Chard, to maintain England's claim on the island. After burying Sir George's heart on St. George's Island, Matthew Somers and the *Patience* party returned to England with his uncle's body, where it was laid to rest in his native Dorsetshire.

The stories of Bermuda told by the *Sea Venture* survivors provoked great excitement among the Virginia Company's "adventurers" (investors or shareholders, in today's parlance). And, to judge by the published accounts written by two of the survivors, William Strachey and Silvester Jourdain, it is easy to see why. Taken together, the reports paint a picture of an island paradise where food was available for the taking, and pearls, tobacco, whales, and ambergris (a whale secretion then used in perfume production), could be had with only a little more effort. Who knew what other treasures Bermuda might hold, what riches it might produce, once the island was properly surveyed and colonized?

Small wonder then, that by June 16, 1612 a group of wealthy and powerful men allied with the Virginia Company had persuaded King James to grant them an extension of the original Virginia charter to cover Bermuda, "for and in consideration of the Sum of two thousand pounds of lawful English money." Or that, a month before the charter had been formally extended, the Company had already dispatched the ship *Plough,* with sixty settlers aboard, to its promising new colony in Bermuda.

Colonial World: Outpost of Empire

The *Plough* and her sixty passengers had an uneventful Atlantic crossing, reaching St. George's on July 11, 1612. Since these were Bermuda's first (intentionally) permanent settlers, it is relevant to ask a simple question: Why had they come?

Today, close to four centuries after Bermuda was founded as a colony, there may be a lack of clarity about, a tendency to romanticize the motivation behind, the founding of colonies in the New World. But, for the Virginia Company, there was no lack of clarity. The Company's letter of instructions to the colony's first governor, Richard Moore, makes it abundantly clear that the Company considered its Bermuda "plantation" a business venture with one purpose—and that purpose was to generate handsome dividends for its shareholders. In the Company's view, the settlers being sent to the colony were the Company's employees, whose job it was to make sure the colony turned a profit. In addition to wages for certain work done, they would be sharecroppers on the land they farmed, paying half their production as rent to the Company. (Perhaps here is a good place to note that in 1615 the Virginia Company transferred control of the colony to the related Somers Island Company. Along with this transfer came a new charter from King James which granted the colonists the right to call a General Assembly to enact local laws.)

Regrettably, the settlers' understanding of their role was not recorded in such a clear and concise fashion. Unlike the colony's shareholders, Bermuda's settlers were people of humble station, and whether they shared and accepted the Company's understanding of their role is uncertain. But it seems likely, based on human nature and subsequent events, that their intentions were less defined

When some of the *Sea Venture* survivors returned to England with glowing accounts of their Bermuda sojourn, the Virginia Company promptly obtained a new royal charter granting it the right to colonize Bermuda as well. In July of 1612 the first sixty colonists arrived, and set to work clearing the land to plant tobacco. The colony's early houses were built of the island's cedar, and thatched with the leaves of the palmetto.

In 1612, the first year of Bermuda's settlement, the colonists founded a town on St. George's Island, at the northeastern tip of Bermuda. Located on a well-protected harbour and easily accessible to ocean-going ships, the town of St. George would remain Bermuda's capital and the center of her commercial and social life for the next two centuries.

and more complex. Quite probably, like immigrants the world over and throughout history, they had a vague notion that the new colony would offer them a fresh start, a better life, both materially and socially, than was their lot in England.

But despite their differences of birth and position, and whatever their understanding, the shareholders back in England and the settlers just arriving in Bermuda had two important things in common. They knew very little about the island, and yet nonetheless they had very high expectations of what it had to offer.

As Lefroy and subsequent writers have noted, the *Sea Venture* survivors who returned to England with their stories of their Bermuda sojourn had no intention of deliberately misleading anyone about the island. But after the bitter desolation of Jamestown, their memories of the island that had been their salvation and idyllic home for most of a year must have been warm indeed. From the written

accounts alone, it is easy to come away with the impression that Bermuda was an Eden where mere subsistence was effortless, and wealth in the form of ambergris, pearls, silk, whale oil, rare woods—even gold, perhaps—could be had with only a little industry. To supplement these windfall riches, the island's moderate climate and fertile soil would surely produce bountiful crops of tobacco, sugar cane, and wine grapes.

Alas, for both the settlers and the shareholders the reality of life in Bermuda would prove decidedly less rosy. The turtles, birds, cedar berries, palmetto berries, and palmetto heart—the entire cornucopia of wild foodstuffs on which the *Sea Venture* survivors had feasted—were a bounty which had built up over thousands of years. The wild hogs, too, introduced by the Spanish, had multiplied for decades without predators.

Now, with the arrival of hundreds of settlers, this natural larder was fast depleted. (Although the colonists could not know it, the introduction of wild hogs in the 1500s had already demonstrated the delicacy of the ecological balance. For the hogs had themselves decimated the cahow population by digging up their underground nests and eating their eggs.) So severe was the human toll on turtles and hogs that in 1620 and 1623 the island's House of Assembly enacted laws to protect them from overhunting.

Worse still, from the Company's point of view, there was very little ambergris, few if any pearls, and no gold at all to be found. Although there were whales in the surrounding ocean, catching them proved difficult and dangerous for the unskilled. And the only wood in any quantity was Bermuda cedar—valuable enough for island furniture, houses, and boats, but not for export. As these disappointing facts set in, it became obvious that any profits the Company might hope for would have to come from the settlers' efforts as farmers.

The Company had decided early on that tobacco would be the colony's cash crop, for tobacco could be easily transported, commanded high prices in England, and was well suited to the island. (Indeed, the account of one *Sea Venture* survivor, Silvester Jourdain, suggests that tobacco grew wild on the island; apparently it had been planted by the Spanish at some time during the 1500s.) But despite the fact that it grew well on the island, tobacco was to prove a commercial disappointment, for it had to compete with the tobacco grown in Virginia, which was greatly superior in quality. To make matters worse, the Company's agents complained that the settlers were keeping the best tobacco back for themselves, and that, due to careless packing, entire shipments rotted before they reached London.

The settlers had their own complaints: they were not happy about being required to grow tobacco (and, in the absence of money, often being paid in it), despite the fact that it could not compete against the Virginia crop. And they complained that many of their fellow settlers, sent out by the Company, were ne'er-do-wells who were both trouble-makers and unwilling to work. Underlying the colonists' grievances was the fact that they saw the shareholders as distant landlords who constantly demanded profits but did not share or understand the hardships of daily life on the island.

Undoubtedly the colonists' biggest single complaint, however, was the Company's insistence on a monopoly over shipping and trading with the colony, a monopoly which the Company considered essential to the colony's profitability. Indeed, from the earliest days of the colony the settlers had shown no great love for the hard work of tilling the soil. Far more appealing was the idea of earning their living on the sea, shipping and trading in the small, fast sloops they had learned to build out of the island's abundant cedar trees. And, despite the

Bermuda had become a slave-holding society within a decade of the colony's founding, a human tragedy which blighted the island's history for over two centuries. The vast majority of the slaves were blacks bought by slave traders on the African coast (as depicted in the print above), and then traded through the West Indies before reaching Bermuda. Though the island lacked the plantation conditions of other New World colonies, slaves were essential to the "Salt, Cedar, and Sailors" economy on which Bermuda prospered throughout the 18th and early 19th centuries.

Although they had been sent to the colony to farm tobacco, Bermudians soon showed themselves to be seafarers at heart. By the end of the 17th century Bermudians had become a dominant force in shipping and trading between the West Indies and North America, and their swift sloops, built from the island's native cedar trees and carrying an enormous sail area, were renowned throughout the seafaring world.

efforts of the Company to prohibit it, this the islanders proceeded to do, at first surreptitiously, then increasingly in the open. Not only was life on the sea easier work than being a sharecropper on the land—it also made it easier to avoid paying a share of the profits to the Company.

A succession of colonial governors were caught in the middle, trying to mediate between profitless shareholders and wayward but unrepentant colonists. What lay at the bottom of the squabbles however, was beyond mediation: the disillusion and disappointment of both the Company and the colonists when the island proved unable to meet their original high expectations. Finally, after some seventy contentious years, the colonists had had enough. After numerous petitions to King Charles II, the Company's charter was forfeited to the Crown in 1684. (Henceforth, the colony's governors would be appointed by the Crown. Nonetheless, the Bermudians' right to legislate their own

Richard DeRosset 1996

Among the colony's earliest public structures were the Anglican churches built in each of the parishes, and over time most of them were rebuilt in the Gothic style favored in the late 18th and the 19th centuries. Two parish churches, however, retain much of the architectural flavor of the early 1700s: St. Peter's Church, the jewel of St. George's [facing page], was founded in 1612, and is the oldest Anglican place of worship in continuous use in the New World. The present building dates from 1713, although it has undergone numerous alterations and additions in the ensuing years.

Unique in retaining an unembellished cottage-style architecture, the Old Devonshire Church [above] was originally built in 1716. After an arson fire destroyed the historic church in 1970, the parish lovingly built this exact replica where the original had stood.

The lack of roads in the early years of the colony meant that goods and people travelled by water, and the island's natural harbours, such as Flatts Inlet, became centers of trade where small villages sprang up [facing page].

During the 18th century, after the colony had grown more prosperous, and the threat posed by hurricanes was better understood, the settlers began replacing their cedar-and-palmetto homes with the stone houses which came to be known as the "Bermuda cottage." A surprising number of these early farmhouses have survived, especially in the western parishes. One of the oldest is Stamp House in Warwick [above], built about 1705, and still in use as a private residence.

laws through their House of Assembly—a right originally granted by King James' charter in 1615—was not surrendered, and thus the island did not become a "Crown Colony.")

"Salt, Cedar, and Sailors" — and Slavery

With the departure of the Somers Island Company, the Company's shipping and trading monopoly so detested by the islanders came to an end. But years before the prohibitions against ship building and ocean trading were formally lifted, a group of Bermudian ship owners were regularly sailing nearly a thousand miles south to tiny Turks Island, where they had, in effect, established a colony of their own, and set up a salt making operation. The salt pans on Turks Island were the foundation for an ocean shipping and trading business which Bermudians operated throughout the West Indies and along the eastern seaboard of North America until well into the 19th century. Salt was raked in the warm months of the year, then carried to American ports where it was sold or bartered for food and other essentials Bermuda had need of. This trade founded on salt so dominated Bermudian life that at one point, over twelve hundred men—then nearly thirty percent of the island's working-age male population—were engaged in the salt trade alone.

So the century and a half beginning about 1678 has been well labeled the era of "Salt, Cedar, and Sailors." But the salt industry, and all that flowed from it, depended on a fourth "s" which has sometimes been overlooked—slavery. For it was Bermudian slaves who did much of the work in the salt pans of Turks Island, and helped man the sloops which carried salt and other goods between the Caribbean and North America.

Slavery had arrived in the colony within the first decade of its settlement, and in accepting slavery Bermuda adopted the pattern of New World colonial slavery first established by the Spanish a hundred years earlier on the island of Hispaniola. The first two decades of the colony saw only a trickle of slaves. But in the following decades so many slaves were being brought to the island that concern was expressed about the colony's ability to employ and support them, and in 1674 the House of Assembly enacted a law prohibiting further slave imports. The vast majority of slaves were black Africans brought from the West Indies, but there were others as well, including a few North American Indians and Scotch and Irish soldiers taken prisoner and sold into slavery in the 1650s, following the English Civil Wars. (Although very few in number, enough American Indian slaves were brought to Bermuda that their bloodlines were seen in some Bermudian visages for decades to follow, especially in some of the families on St. David's Island.)

Histories of the colony repeatedly make two points about slavery in Bermuda: first, that because the island lacked plantation conditions, there was no economic justification for slavery in the colony; and, second, that the conditions of Bermudian slavery were milder than those which existed in other slave-holding areas.

It is true that in Bermuda there were no plantations such as those that existed in the American South and on the islands of the West Indies. But from 1678 on, Bermuda did maintain a plantation economy—on Turks Island, a thousand miles to the south, where the "crop" was salt, rather than sugar or cotton. And the first point also overlooks the universal and fundamental motivation for slavery: human laziness and greed. For even without plantations, slaves were a cheap labor force for work around the house or garden, and slave owners routinely hired out their slaves to others as wage laborers. (The general practice was to allow the slave to retain a portion—typically one third—of such wages earned, while the slave owner pocketed the balance.)

As to the second point, however, the evidence appears overwhelming that Bermudian slavery was in fact milder than in places such as the American South and the larger West Indian islands. Because Bermuda is so small and most slave owners had only a few slaves, most Bermudian slaves lived in close proximity to their owners, and often worked side-by-side with their masters and other whites. A high proportion of Bermudian slaves were skilled laborers, many working in shipyards and aboard ships as seamen, for example. (Even the slaves who worked half the year in the salt pans of the Turks Islands spent the rest of the year aboard their masters' ships, or back in Bermuda.) And despite the picture suggested by the title of one book on Bermudian slavery, physical confinement or the use of manacles and chains was essentially unheard of—although perhaps superfluous as well, since on such a small island a slave's chances of escape were practically nil.

Nonetheless, the fact remains that once their workday was over, slaves in Bermuda could generally go about their private lives unfettered. (Although this liberty of movement would be severely restricted for a time in the wake of the several slave plots which were uncovered during the 17th and 18th centuries.) All of these factors helped to create an environment in which whites and slaves were in constant contact, often came to know each other quite well, and in which the cruelty toward slaves which characterized some slave-holding societies was rare.

Although there is evidence that conditions for Bermuda's slaves improved over the course of the slave era, nothing in Bermuda's record of slavery suggests that Bermuda's slaves were happy with their lot. The island's many failed slave uprisings alone are clear evidence to the contrary: as many as seven hundred slaves were implicated in the 1761 conspiracy, for example. And there is no record of a young, able-bodied slave ever refusing freedom through manumission. (In arguing the benevolence of Bermudian slavery, mention is sometimes made of the cases in which Bermudian slaves declined freedom when the ships on which they were working docked in countries where slavery was illegal. But it must be noted that in such cases freedom meant starting life over with nothing in a strange country, and came at the enormous price of forever abandoning family, home, and friends in Bermuda.)

American Trade and Troubles

After the ouster of the Somers Island Company, Bermudians were at last free to pursue their first love: the sea. In addition to ocean trading, they also turned to fishing and whaling, and, during England's recurring wars with France and Spain, privateering as well. All this seafaring required boats and ships, and the fast, light sloops built of Bermuda cedar were soon in demand all over the Atlantic. By the early 18th century, shipbuilding had become an important island industry.

The reason why Bermudians developed such a passion for life on the sea can only be guessed at. It may have been a reaction to the Company's shipping monopoly and incessant demands for agricultural production. Perhaps the island's small size fostered a desire for wider horizons which only the sea could fulfill. Perhaps some could foresee that a small island devoid of natural resources could never provide all her people's material wants, and that Bermudians would have to trade if they were to prosper. Or it could be that work on the sea was

Bermudians' fortunes rose with the blossoming of sea trading in the 18th century, and they began building houses befitting their new station. Many of these grand homes are found in Paget and Warwick Parishes, overlooking Hamilton Harbour and the Great Sound. Blackburn Place [above] dates from 1730, although, like many other historic houses, it has been added to over the years. The house was the ancestral home of the seafaring Darrell family, which gave its name to Darrell's Wharf, just across Harbour Road from Blackburn Place.

Another of the grand houses built during the heyday of seafaring is Spithead [above], built in the late 1700s. It occupies a point of land jutting into the Great Sound at Granaway Deep, and few Bermuda homes can claim a more spectacular site. Legendary privateer Hezekiah Frith reputedly built Spithead here because he could anchor his ships behind Spithead Point, out of view of Hamilton's customs officials!

As Bermuda's population and commerce grew, pressure mounted to relocate the capital of the colony nearer the center of the island. In 1793 a settlement on the north shore of Crow Lane Harbour (as the eastern extremity of the Great Sound was then called), was incorporated as the town of Hamilton. Two decades later, despite the fierce opposition of the St. Georgians, and one year before Captain Brown of the British Army's 100th Regiment executed his lovely drawing of Hamilton as it was in 1816 [facing page], the seat of government was transferred from St. George's to the rapidly growing new town. In 1838 the Public Building [above] was erected in the new capital to house government offices. Known today as the Cabinet Building, the handsome structure stands in a lovely park on Front Street.

simply more fun and less like drudgery than tilling Bermuda's small farm plots. Whatever the reason, when Bermudians took to the sea they set the island on a course which would forever alter its destiny. For it led to the creation of a collective Bermudian "personality" which was open to the outside world, welcoming of new ideas, products, and people. Over the longer term, it meant that Bermudians, though island dwellers, would never become an insular people.

The more immediate result was a strengthening of Bermuda's bonds with the English colonies of North America. Those ties, based on family and friendships, dated from the earliest years of the Jamestown settlement, and when the English presence spread along the Atlantic seaboard during the 17th and early 18th centuries, the Bermudian connection spread with it. Much of this Bermudian connection grew out of emigration to North America and the natural affinity between colonials, but what really bound Bermuda and America were the commercial relationships created as Bermudians traded salt and other goods up and down the American coast. Those commercial ties grew to be of critical importance to Bermuda, for as their sea pursuits prospered, Bermudians increasingly neglected the island's agriculture: by the 1770s three quarters of Bermuda's food was being imported from the American colonies.

So when the American Revolutionary War erupted in 1775, Bermudians found themselves in a perilous position, and with divided loyalties. Most islanders had no wish to join the Thirteen Colonies in seeking independence, but many Bermudians felt a deep sympathy with their American cousins, not least of all because of their vital trade links with America.

An incident which came to be known as the Gunpowder Plot, and its aftermath, reflects the deep divisions in loyalties which existed on the island. With the outbreak of the war, Great Britain's colonies, including Bermuda, were forbidden to trade with the rebellious Americans, and the American Continental Congress likewise forbade trade with British territory. Bermudians were torn: they were loyal to their Mother Country, but if Bermuda could not trade with America, the island faced starvation. A Bermudian delegation was sent to the Continental Congress to plead for special consideration; it returned home after being advised that George Washington's army was as starved for gunpowder as the island was for food. Then, on the night of August 15, 1775, a hundred barrels of gunpowder were stolen from the St. George's powder magazine and transferred in whaleboats to a waiting American frigate. The perpetrators, who undoubtedly counted some Bermudians among their number, were never caught, and shortly thereafter, a grateful Continental Congress allowed trade with the island to resume. But despite the American decision to resume trade, some Bermudian shipowners, perhaps more loyal to Britain—and perhaps less concerned with the island's fortunes than their own—seized the opportunity of the war to begin privateering against American shipping.

After the loss of her Thirteen Colonies, and the outbreak of the French Revolutionary Wars in the 1790s, Britain began to see Bermuda's mid-Atlantic location in a new strategic light. Small contingents of British soldiers had been stationed on the island from time to time since the early 1700s, but from the 1790s on Britain began to build Bermuda into "the Gibraltar of the West." In 1810, construction began on a massive naval dockyard on Ireland Island, a project which would continue for decades and employ hundreds of men at a time. The construction of the dockyard, together with the sizeable naval and military forces stationed on the island, would constitute a major element in the life

Bermuda's encircling reefs, which had plagued shipping from the 16th century, remained just as deadly three centuries later, and in 1846 Gibbs Hill Lighthouse was erected atop Gibbs Hill in Southampton. Its rotating beam is visible to ships forty miles out to sea, and each year thousands of tourists climb its 185 steps for the glorious view from the top.

In the first half of the 1860s, during America's Civil War, St. George's Harbour filled with ships using Bermuda as an entre-pôt for running the Northern blockade of the Confederacy's ports. Blockade-running was to prove the last hurrah for Bermuda's maritime tradition, which had been in de-cline since the abolition of slavery. When the Civil War boom years ended, Bermudi-ans had no choice but to seek their fortunes in their land and their own inner resources.

and economy of Bermuda until the mid-twenti-eth century. (Britain's decision to strengthen Bermuda as a military outpost was also influ-enced by the potential for further hostilities with the fledgling United States of America, a con-cern which later became reality in the War of 1812. Even during the Revolutionary War, the Continental Congress had toyed with the idea of sending a force to invade and annex Bermuda.)

The End of an Era

Even before America's Revolutionary War, anoth-er central socio-economic element of Bermudian life—slavery—had begun to come under fire. The overt attacks on slavery came from abroad, as abolitionists increasingly gained a hearing and political power in Britain. In 1772 slavery was abolished within the British Isles, and from that point on, the abolitionist forces in the British Par-liament were on the march against slavery

Richard DeRosset, 1986

throughout the British Empire. In Bermuda itself, the earliest open attacks on slavery came from visiting Methodist missionaries at the end of the 18th century. With the arrival of these missionaries, large numbers of slaves were converted to Christianity, for in Bermuda, as in all the British colonies, the Anglican Church had historically denied baptism to the slaves. Then, in 1807, the abolitionists achieved their intermediate goal when the British Parliament abolished the slave trade throughout the Empire, a move widely understood to presage the abolition of slavery itself.

But if the overt attacks came from abroad, the fact is that within Bermuda itself the moral and economic underpinnings of slavery had also begun to crumble. The psychological foundation for slavery rested on the belief that slaves were different, subhuman; and in the early days of slavery the condition of slaves newly arrived from Africa or a foreign colony made that belief all the easier to hold. They were black, and from a vastly different culture; perhaps most important of all, they spoke little or no English, and so could not understand, or be understood by, the white world around them. But as the years passed, Bermuda's slave population changed: of necessity, they learned English and adapted to English culture. The barriers to communication and understanding gradually fell; and as they did, whites began to realize that their slaves were human beings in a darker skin.

As the eighteenth century drew to a close the economic basis for Bermuda's slavery was disappearing as well. In 1799 the Bahamas took control of Turks Island, and from that point onward Bermuda's salt industry—and the need for slaves to work the salt pans—was in decline. To make matters worse, in 1822 Britain opened its West Indian ports to American ships, bringing new competition to Bermudian ship owners, and further reducing the need for slaves at sea.

Given this moral and economic evolution, it is hardly surprising that toward the end of the eighteenth century the freeing, or manumission, of slaves became increasingly common. After 1820 manumissions again increased substantially, so that by the year prior to emancipation, Bermuda's population included one "free coloured" for every three slaves.

And so when the British Parliament acted to abolish slavery throughout the Empire as of August 1, 1834, Bermuda was ready to move on. After more than two centuries, a long and lamentable period in the island's history had come to an end. Emancipation did not, of course, mean instant equality, and racial discrimination remained an element of Bermudian life until well into the middle of the twentieth century. But the nature of Bermudian slavery did make it easier for Bermuda to evolve, over the course of the next one hundred and fifty years, into a racially harmonious and truly democratic society.

Steamships and Civil War

In the spring of 1834, as Bermuda counted down to Emancipation Day, a ship appeared off Bermuda's coast and took a turn around Hamilton Harbour. Although Bermudians were used to seeing ships, the *Marco Bozzaris* caused a great deal of excitement, for it was the first steam-powered ship ever to enter Bermuda's waters. But among the more thoughtful of the onlookers there must have been some melancholy mixed with that excitement, for they realized that they were witnessing the beginning of the end of another era. For with the coming of steam, and the iron and steel hulls it would power, the days of sail and wooden ships were destined to fade away. And the days of Bermuda's shipbuilding industry, built on the island's famous cedar, were destined to fade away as well.

The age of sail did not vanish immediately, nor without a fight. In response to the challenge of steam, shipbuilders the world over produced the fastest and most beautiful wooden sailing ships of all time—the clippers. As late as the 1850s and '60s, Bermuda's master shipwrights crafted such famous clippers as the *Pearl* and the *Kohinoor*, which, given good winds, could trounce the early steamers. But in the world of shipping, a dependable arrival is worth far more than an extra knot or two, and the steam-driven paddle-wheelers, though squat and ungainly compared with the sleek clippers, did not have to wait for the wind. By the 1860s, the contest was almost over, and the harbors of the world were full of steamships.

* * *

From the summer of 1861 until the closing days of 1864, little St. George's Harbour was as crowded with steamships as any port in the world.

When the Civil War broke out in America in April of 1861, the North imposed a blockade of the Confederacy's ports, and Queen Victoria imposed a strict neutrality on all British subjects. But, blockade or no, the South had need of munitions and food, and England's cotton mills still had need of cotton from their traditional suppliers, the plantations of the American South. Bermuda, of course, had historic sympathies with Virginia and other Southern States. Bermuda also had a geographic location in the western Atlantic that was a blockade-runner's dream. And lastly the island had, despite the royal proclamation, buccaneering sea captains, shipowners, and sailors ready to chance their luck against the blockade if there was big money to be made.

And there *was* big money to be made: for a single run to a Confederate port and back, a seaman could make two hundred and fifty dollars; captains and pilots, five thousand dollars. For the owner, profits were so great that his ship was paid for after just two successful runs.

Bermuda was the entrepôt: since it was a neutral port, larger, slower ships could make the passage between Bermuda and England without fear of Union ships on blockade patrol. At St. George's the cargoes would be transferred to and from the small, fast steamers which made the runs into the Confederate ports.

For three and a half phenomenal years the island overflowed with ships, sailors, war talk, and money. Bermuda had seen nothing like it since the War of 1812, when her privateers had had their "last hurrah" against American shipping. That half century between wars had seen a slow decline in the island's fortunes, as her carrying trade and shipyards faded. At times during those quiet, sometimes desperate, decades, only the money flowing into the Royal Navy's dockyard and the British military forces stationed on the island had kept the economy afloat. But now, with the Civil War, the good times were back. Once again, as in the old days, Bermudians were masters of the sea, and the sea was bringing Bermuda good fortune.

And then, after nearly four terrible years of war, the Confederacy fell.

Bermudian World

The blockade-running that fueled Bermuda's life and economy at high speed for nearly four years came to a halt in the final days of 1864 as the Confederacy crumbled. As with all speculative bubbles, to the very end those in the game heard nothing but good news, and it seemed the good times would roll on forever. The island's shipping capacity had been expanded, and expanded again, to meet the demand of the boom. Local merchants had built up large inventories of goods, much of it bought on credit, to supply the needs of the ships and crews crowding the island. And so when the Confederacy fell and, almost overnight, the blockade-running ships and their crews vanished, Bermuda's economy also fell, and fell hard.

In fact the island's maritime economy had been in decline for decades, and had it not been for the money flowing from the British Treasury into military construction and payrolls, the island would have been in desperate straits. From 1799 on, the Turks Island salt pans and the trading based on salt were gradually lost to Bahamian interests. With the build-up of the island into a strong mid-Atlantic military outpost since the early years of the nineteenth century, Bermuda's enterprising privateers had been put out of work, their role supplanted by the Royal Navy. Then, in 1822, pressure from her West Indian colonies forced Britain to relax the historic Navigation Acts and open those Caribbean ports to American vessels, which meant increasing competition for Bermudian ships. With the loss of slave labor after emancipation in 1834, the wages of seamen had risen, further worsening the competitive position of Bermudian shipowners. But above all, the iron-hulled steamship, built in the shipyards of Europe and America, had been displacing Bermuda's cedar-built sloops and ships and, of course, forcing the island's shipwrights into retirement as well.

The island's agriculture, too, suffered after emancipation. Farming had been so disdained from the earliest days of the colony that even among Bermuda's slaves farm work was despised, considered fit only for the very old and infirm.

Front Street, Hamilton, Bermuda.

As their maritime industries declined throughout the nineteenth century and especially following the American Civil War, Bermudians were forced to seek their livelihood in other ways. With the help of Portuguese farmers who had immigrated from the Azores, the island turned to farming vegetables for export. Ironically, it was the steamship, which had made Bermuda's wooden sailing ships obsolete, which now provided the reliable transport to the New York market, and by the late nineteenth century, wagons loaded with produce crowding Front Street [above] on the fortnightly "steamer days" had become a common sight.

View from Gibbs Hill

In the decades following the Civil War, wealthy, winter-shy American visitors discovered Bermuda's balmy climate, rural quiet, and quiet beauty, and with the arrival of these intrepid early visitors, Bermuda's era of tourism was born. The classic view looking northeast from Gibbs Hill Lighthouse [facing page] exemplifies Bermuda's storied combination of verdant island, blue water, and picturesque houses, and a postcard from the 1920s [above] provides an idea of the changes which have come to the island over the past few decades.

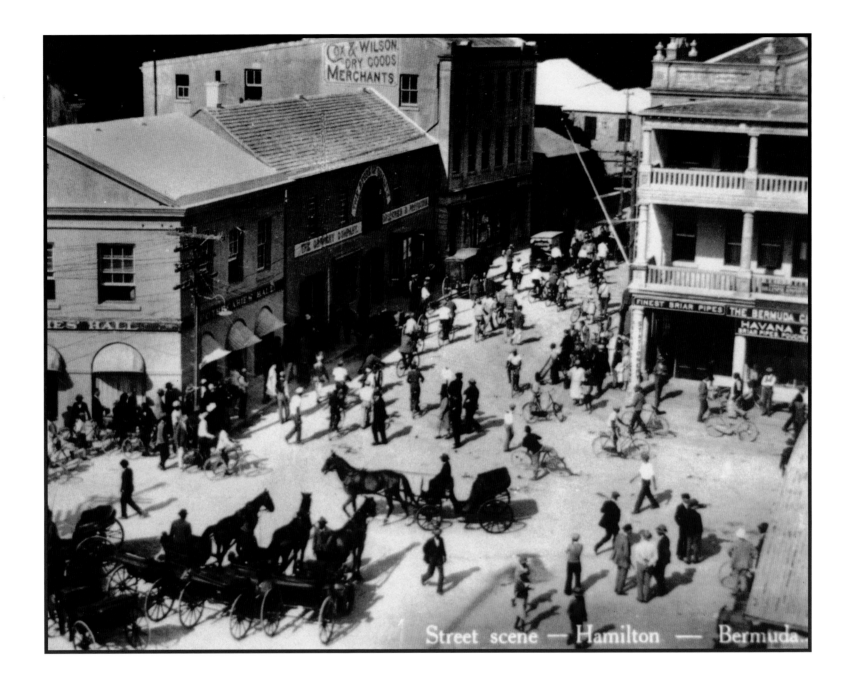

From the end of the nineteenth century, advances in transportation and communications were shrinking the world and transforming Bermuda's world as well. By the 1920s, luxury steamships were bringing tens of thousands of visitors to the island each year, making tourism the most important sector of the economy. Then, in 1937, came commercial air service, and the magnificent "Flying Boats", using the Great Sound as their landing strip, cut travel time to New York from days to hours.

But in this transportation picture, as in the historic pictures of Front Street from the 1930s *[caption continues on facing page]*

shown on these pages, one element was missing: the automobile. For in 1908 the island's legislature had prohibited the use of motor vehicles, and Bermuda remained steadfastly car-less until
the 1940s. Lacking cars, Bermudians travelled by foot, horse, bicycle, and, after 1931, by train:
nicknamed "Rattle and Shake", the single-track railroad ran the length of Bermuda, from St.
George's to Somerset. [The picture on the left-hand page shows the intersection of Front and
Queen Streets, known to Bermudians as Heyl's Corner, where the "Birdcage" now stands; the picture on the right-hand page looks eastward along Front Street.]

Thus it is hardly surprising that after emancipation, when farm labor could no longer be compelled, the result was that farmland lay fallow for want of anyone willing to till the fields. Farming was in such a sorry state by 1839 that newly-arrived Governor William Reid was shocked to find only two serviceable plows in all of Bermuda, and among the highest priorities of that very active governor was the development of the island's agriculture. (In the decades following the Civil War, the island's government would later act on one of Governor Reid's recommendations when it encouraged the immigration of Portuguese farmers from the Azores.)

The Onion Patch

Given this historic aversion to working the soil, it was assuredly only out of necessity that in the mid-19th century Bermudians turned to farming in a substantial way. No doubt partly due to Governor Reid's prodding, in the twenty-five years leading up to the Civil War, farm acreage tripled and agricultural exports, including celery, tomatoes, arrowroot, and, especially, potatoes and onions, became an important part of Bermuda's economy.

After the war, regular steamer service to New York would further expand these exports of early vegetables, and the island's onions would become so famous overseas that Bermuda would come to be known as "the Onion Patch" and Bermudians as "Onions"—affectionate nicknames which have remained with them to this day.

It is ironic, of course, that the nicknames Bermuda and her people acquired should link them with the very activity Bermudians had so long held in such low esteem. But, coming when they did, these nicknames were not as inappropriate as they might seem. For although Bermudians had yearned to make their living on the sea from the earliest years of the colony, with the coming of the steam era the time when Bermuda could subsist on sea and sail had come to an end. And so, while that love for the sea and interest in the world over the horizon were not about to die, over the next few decades Bermudians would increasingly turn their attention to their "Onion Patch"—and to the magnificent world their tiny island held within its narrow shores.

They were not alone: for the outside world was also beginning to discover the island's tranquil beauty and the mild winter climate which Bermudians themselves had so long taken for granted. It was the visit in 1884 of Princess Louise, daughter of Queen Victoria and wife of the Governor-General of Canada, which put Bermuda on the map for winter excursions in an age before "tourism" existed. But the Princess, although certainly the most eminent early visitor, had been preceded by a good many others: indeed, a few intrepid visitors had come in sailing ships before the Civil War. Partly in response to those early visitors, the island's first sizeable hotel, the Hamilton, was begun in 1852, although it would not be completed until eleven years later, during the Civil War boom years.

But it was the dependable (even though, initially, less comfortable) steamer that transformed an adventure for the plucky into a routine ocean passage, and in the late 1860s more and more people in search of an escape from harsh winter weather began riding the produce steamships on their return journey south from New York. Mark Twain arrived in 1867, on the first of many visits, and found Bermuda already "the tidiest place in the world." In 1874 travel to the island became more elegant and comfortable when twice-monthly passenger steamship service began, and a decade later the Princess Hotel, named in honor of Princess Louise's visit, opened on Hamilton Harbour. These early years were hardly a tourism gold rush: there were only about two thousand visitors in 1889, for example. But by the closing decades of the nineteenth century, the seeds that would blossom into Bermuda's twentieth-century visitor industry had been well planted.

No Place Is an Island

The steamship, whose coming had spelled the end of Bermuda's maritime era, did more than transport the island's vegetables north and winter visitors south. By creating reliable connections to Europe and America, it radically altered Bermuda's relationship with the outside world. No longer was Bermuda an uncertain, exotic destination which might be reached sometime in the indefinite future; with dependable steam propulsion ships could depart and arrive on a schedule. Cargo and passenger traffic mushroomed as a result. And it was not only visitors who were taking advantage of steamer travel: growing numbers of Bermudians began travelling abroad for business, pleasure, and schooling, and in the process were exposed to new ideas, new products, and other ways of living.

Of course the steamship was just the leading edge of a flood of new technology sweeping over the planet, and by tying Bermuda ever closer to the outside world, these technological advances would open that outside world to Bermudians and transform the island world Bermudians had known since the 17th century. In 1887 telephone service within the island began. Two years later an undersea telegraph cable to Halifax cut the time required to communicate with the island from days to mere seconds, despite some anxiety that visitors would object to being at the mercy of constant telegrams. It would not be the last time that concerns for the visitor industry would deter the adoption of new technology: in 1908, after an early and regretted experience with that new, noisy, and smelly beast—the automobile—the island's legislature would pro-hibit their use on the island's public roads. For the time being, Bermudians would get around by foot, horse, and bicycle. Nonetheless, by 1931 Bermudians apparently had become comfortable with telecommunications, since no serious objection was raised to the new transoceanic telephone cable when it was inaugurated that year.

Partly as a result of these contacts abroad, education on the island was expanded and formalized: most of the island's oldest schools, including Whitney Institute, Saltus Grammar School, Mount St. Agnes Academy, Bermuda High School for Girls, and Berkeley Institute, date from the 1880s and '90s. And the oldest school in Bermuda, Warwick Academy, which had been founded in 1662, was substantially expanded shortly thereafter.

All of this travel and visiting resulted in two additional social trends: increasingly, Bermuda's contacts were with America and Americans, rather than with the Mother Country. Of course, the Bermuda-American connection was nothing new; it had begun in the early 1600s. But during the era of sail it was mostly sailors who visited America; with the coming of the steamship, many more Bermudians, and from all walks of life, travelled abroad, and Americans on holiday became a common fixture of Bermuda's winter season. (In the 1920s, according to the travel writer Hudson Strode, the island's British expatriates were already needling Bermudians about the Americanization of the island.) With all of this social interaction, Bermudians were increasingly marrying Americans, and to a lesser extent, Canadians, further strengthening old social, cultural, and economic bonds. Somewhat later, another connection was strengthened by an increasing number of intermarriages between Bermudians and West Indians, many of whom had travelled to Bermuda for work opportunities.

Agriculture remained the most important sector of the economy for the first two decades of the 20th century, but in the decade following World

As the Second World War ended and the Cold War began, Bermuda's strategic location remained vital to NATO defenses, and the islanders soon grew accustomed to seeing the U.S. Navy's P-3 Orions returning from submarine-hunting patrols to their base on St. David's Island [above]. On the ground, a surging post-war economy, coupled with Bermudians' newly acquired access to motor vehicles, led to a building boom which gradually spread the population and housing—historically concentrated around Hamilton and St. George's—to every corner of the island. [On the facing page, an aerial view over Devonshire looking eastward along the south shore.]

The world-wide economic boom of the post-war era ushered in a new era of mass tourism for Bermuda. Safe, inexpensive air travel made the difference, and transformed Bermuda from a winter into a summer resort—for now tourists in search of a break from snow and frost could easily jet to the tropical warmth of the Caribbean. Bermuda, on the other hand, just two hours from New York and with gorgeous stretches of sand like Windsor Beach [above] and half a dozen superb golf courses, like Castle Harbour [facing page], became just the place for a week-long, or even a long weekend, summer getaway.

Car-less until 1946, Bermudians took to the motor vehicle with astonishing speed, swiftly dashing the (perhaps self-serving) predictions during the end-the-car-ban debates that, due to the expense, there would never be more than 500 private cars on the island. That figure, alas, had been surpassed within a year; by 1993 there were over 20,000.

That figure would be much higher were it not for a law restricting car ownership to one per household, and prohibiting tourists from driving cars at all. As a result, Bermuda is to a large extent a two-wheeled society, and the island counts roughly as many mopeds, scooters, and motorcycles as cars.

The tugboat *Powerful* stands by while a cruise ship makes ready to sail from St. George's. After being nearly eclipsed by air travel, arriving in Bermuda by sea had a rebirth when vacationing by cruise ship began to take off in the 1970s.

War I, luxury steamship service and new tourist facilities, including the island's first two golf courses, pushed tourism into first place. (America's adoption of prohibition in 1920 no doubt helped as well, since vacationing Americans could of course drink alcohol openly in Bermuda.) These early decades of the century were a gilded era for Bermuda's tourism, the era when the rich, famous, and powerful adopted Bermuda as "their" special island, free of the hustle and hassle of urban, industrial America. Woodrow Wilson was a visitor before he became President (he added his name to a petition of prominent Americans who were opposed to the introduction of the motor-car into the island); President William Howard Taft visited in 1920, after his term in office (he wrote an article for the *National Geographic Magazine* about his month-long visit). And everyone praised the island for its beauty and its peace and quiet, where the loudest noises were the clip-clop of horses' hooves and the tinkling of bicycle bells. Despite the tremendous expansion of tourism, farm exports continued to be an important part of the island's economy until the Great Depression of the 1930s, when America im-

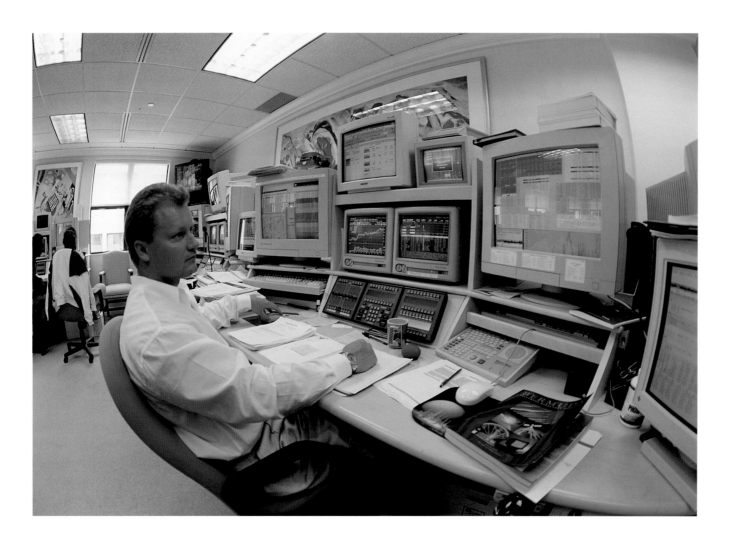

Bermuda is so identified with tourism that many are surprised to learn that a sector broadly termed "international business" now surpasses tourism in its importance to the island's economy. Since the late 1940s, thousands of foreign-based international companies have made the island their corporate "home", drawn by Bermuda's political stability and legal, financial, and tax climate.

With the arrival of the "information age", an array of companies involved in financial services [such as the investment management firm pictured above] have discovered that those same factors, coupled with the island's excellent telecommunications, air connections, and living conditions, make Bermuda a superb operations center as well. The island has proved especially attractive to the insurance industry, and by the mid-1990s, dozens of international firms, specializing in the captive and reinsurance aspects of the market, were running their worldwide operations from Bermuda [the facing page shows the dramatic atrium of one building housing several such insurance firms].

posed high import duties on agricultural products in an attempt to protect her own farmers.

A War, and After

Bermuda's famed peace and quiet were to be shattered in 1939, when Europe again descended into war, and Bermudians again demonstrated their staunch devotion to their Mother Country, as they had done during the Great War. Bermuda's young men did so by volunteering to fight in units sent overseas, as their fathers had done a generation before. But in the twenty years since World War I, the world had become much smaller: this time Bermuda itself would be asked to sacrifice in the battle against Britain's enemies. Britain needed armaments of war, and America needed bases in the Caribbean and Atlantic to defend her shores. A "lend-lease" arrangement was agreed to, and Bermudians were asked to give up more than one square mile of their tiny island—more than five percent of the total land area—on which to build American bases. The lion's share of the sacrifice fell on the people of St. David's, when in 1941 half of their island was taken over to make way for a new U.S. Army airfield.

With the island's economy heavily dependent on tourism, now devastated by the outbreak of the war, widespread unemployment and privation were anticipated. Due to the shortage and uncertainty of shipping, rationing was implemented, and Bermuda soon came to resemble an armed camp, as hundreds of American and British servicemen put the island on a war footing. But the loss of tourism employment caused by war-time conditions was compensated to a large extent by war-time employment itself: in the construction of military facilities and in staffing a huge mail-censorship operation (housed in the basement of the Princess Hotel) to examine letters and parcels passing between Europe and America.

Although the island served as a base of operations throughout the war, like the rest of the Western Hemisphere, it was fortunate enough to be spared actual enemy attack. What could not be spared was the attack on Bermuda's famed tranquility: throughout the war, military jeeps and trucks roared the length and breadth of the island. At war's end, the island's transportation system was in a shambles: horses had died for lack of feed; bicycles, wagons, and carriages were falling apart due to a lack of spare parts; and the island's tiny railroad was just about beyond repair. Against this war-ravaged backdrop, and after another fierce war—this time of public opinion—in September of 1946 Bermuda decided to "join the great commonplace," as one anguished commentator put it, and voted to permit the general use of motor vehicles.

As with previous technological advances, the opposition to motor vehicles had been linked to their effect on the island's tourist industry. But with the end of the war, a new era of tourism had dawned. America had a population of millions with an unprecedented prosperity and a desire for goods and travel which had been denied them during the war years; and the post-war era saw the advent of large, long-range airplanes (themselves a product of war-time technological advances) which could reach Bermuda in less than three hours. The result was the beginning of an era of mass tourism, tourists who came to the island for a week, rather than a month, and who found Bermuda's newly-imported mopeds just the thing for zipping around the island.

America's masses were not the only ones with pent-up demands. Bermuda's working class, black and white, had gone off to war to fight for freedom and democracy too, just as had the sons of the island's governing class. They came back to a

Bermuda still governed very much as it had been a century earlier, and where only a small minority of the population, the (overwhelmingly white) owners of property, could vote or hold public office. (Bermuda's women had just obtained the right to vote in 1944.) For though slavery had ended on August 1, 1834, no one would have suggested that equality or democracy in the normal sense of the word had arisen after Emancipation Day. Bermuda remained very much a racially- and class-divided society, and stiff property-ownership requirements for the franchise and political office were sure to keep it so.

The battle against this oligarchical system had begun during the war itself, when Dr. Edgar Fitzgerald Gordon, a black Trinidadian immigrant, had begun organizing efforts among Bermuda's workers, and had founded the Bermuda Workers' Association. After the crisis of the war had passed, the Workers' Association called a dock strike and a petition was sent to London protesting Bermuda's social, political, and economic conditions. Change did not come overnight, nor without strife: but after a series of boycotts and strikes, the age-old patterns of segregation began breaking down in the late 1950s. In 1961 the property qualification for voting was eliminated, and two years later Bermuda's first political party was organized. Although electoral refinements would continue into the 1970s, the island's political transformation—from paternalistic oligarchy to representative, responsible government based on one-person, one vote—was largely completed by 1968, when Bermuda adopted its first written Constitution. In terms of governmental organization, the Constitution essentially formalized what had become reality: Bermuda governed itself under its elected House of Assembly, led by the head of the majority party, the Government Leader (a title since changed to Premier). Despite a world-wide trend of colonies seeking independence, Bermuda chose to remain a British colony, and the Governor, appointed by and representing the Crown, now had a largely ceremonial role, although he stood always ready to provide wise counsel whenever it might be sought.

The Switzerland of the Atlantic

Although the first decades after World War II were dominated by tourism, the island was also beginning to attract visitors who were as interested in the island's political stability and legal, financial, and tax climate as they were in the island's scenic beauty and balmy weather. Even before the war, a handful of foreign companies had established their corporate headquarters in Bermuda, attracted by the island's stable political system, British legal tradition, and the absence of a personal or corporate income tax. (During the war itself, when a Nazi invasion of Switzerland was a very real threat, one large Swiss pharmaceutical company incorporated a "stand-by" company in Bermuda, identical in structure to the Swiss original. Had the worst occurred, the Bermuda company could have been activated at a moment's notice to assume control of the company's world-wide business operations.)

In the decades following the war, thousands of foreign-owned "exempted" companies (referring to their exemption from Bermudian taxation and regulations affecting locally-operating businesses) would follow suit, establishing their legal seat in the island. Then, beginning in the 1970s and expanding many times over in the '80s, the island became a base for captive insurance companies, reinsurance companies, and financial services firms, attracted not only by the regulatory, legal, and tax climate, but by Bermuda's superb telecommunications, geographic proximity to New York, and highly educated work force. By the late 1980s,

Like many remote communities, Bermuda has a long tradition of providing its own cultural diversions, and boasts a remarkable number of theatre, music, and dance groups for
a community its size. The community is especially supportive of young people in the arts,
such as these dancers from the Somerset Dance Troupe staging a recital in Hamilton's
City Hall Theatre [above], and dramatist Dwayne Saunders and choreographer Suzette
Harvey [facing page], whose original production "Reality Street", debuted in 1995.

Boasting a fine collection focussing on the island's seafaring past, the Bermuda Maritime Museum is housed at the old Royal Naval Dockyard on Ireland Island. Over the course of the 19th century British convict labor built the Dockyard, including the Queen's Exhibition Hall seen above (it was originally a powder magazine). The Dockyard was converted to civilian uses in the early 1950s when Britain withdrew her naval forces.

Members of the Council and staff of the Bermuda National Trust pose before Waterville, the Trust's historic headquarters located at the foot of Hamilton Harbour. Founded in 1970 and now counting some 3500 members, the Trust is Bermuda's most powerful voice for the preservation of the island's architectural and cultural heritage, as well as its premier environmental organization.

this "international business," to use the all-encompassing term, had surpassed tourism in its importance to the island's economy.

By the end of the seventies the combination of mass tourism and international business had made Bermuda a very wealthy island: in 1984, World Bank figures placed Bermudians' per capita income among the ten highest in the world. And the money flowing into the island was well distributed across the population: by 1979, half the population owned their own homes, a very high figure by world standards, but one that would nonetheless continue rising during the 1980s.

This high level of home ownership had not existed prior to the Second World War: before the introduction of motor vehicles, much of the island's population had been concentrated around Hamilton. As late as the 1940s, Southampton Parish, for example, was still largely farmland; and even in the early 1950s, Bermuda's was a predominantly rural landscape. But the arrival of the motor vehicle, and the post-war surge in wealth, resulted in a building boom and the spread of the population throughout Bermuda. By the end of the sixties, with no end to the construction boom in sight, Bermudians woke up to the fact that their island was being covered over with buildings. (The boom in the number of Bermudians travelling by air no doubt had a role in this awakening: due to the island's lush vegetation and hilly topography, only from an aerial vantage point is the extent of the island's urbanization really apparent.)

Faced with the alarming prospect that the island could eventually lose all of its open space, the government imposed increasingly stringent planning controls. In the private sector, a group of concerned citizens organized the Bermuda National Trust (loosely modeled on the National Trust in Britain) to preserve not only open spaces, but the island's historic architecture as well. In time, it would count some 3500 members, and come to be regarded as the island's most powerful voice and instrument for the preservation of Bermuda's environmental and architectural heritage.

An overbuilt island was perhaps the most visible, but far from the only problem Bermuda faced as it neared the end of the twentieth century. Like nearly every part of the world around it, Bermuda has had to deal with illegal drugs and crime. When these problems arrived in Bermuda, they seemed to do so with special force, perhaps because until very recently many thought that Bermuda's small-town nature made it immune to these two scourges of the modern era. And again, like much of the world around them, Bermudians have become increasingly concerned about the issues affecting the environment, such as global warming and pollution—issues of particular gravity for a tiny country surrounded by an ocean.

The problems besetting the island have no easy solutions, and indeed the island's motto *Quo Fata Ferunt*—"Wherever the fates may carry us"—recognizes that fortune has always played its role in the lives of men and nations. But as far as the problems within her control are concerned, no one need wonder whether Bermuda will emerge from them triumphantly. For in the final analysis, the future of a country is in the hands of her people. Nearly four hundred years ago the first Bermudian settlers landed on Bermuda, bearing with them little more than their resourcefulness. And the tiny island they had chosen had little to offer them but its lush beauty and its strength against a capricious sea. Poor in resources, but rich in resourcefulness, over the course of four centuries the people of Bermuda have forged a land and a way of life that is the envy of the world. Given a little generosity from the fates, no one can doubt that they will continue to do so for many centuries to come.

Bermudiana

Links to an African heritage, members of a gombey "crowd" wait for
their signal to take center stage during an annual dance competition.

A trio of barristers pause during a court recess to pose for the camera on the verandah of the Sessions House, home to Bermuda's Supreme Court. Their robes and wigs reflect the British tradition underpinning Bermuda's legal system, and much of Bermudian life in general. Indeed, there can be no doubt that the people of Bermuda cherish their ties to the Mother Country: in a 1995 referendum on independence, Bermudians voted overwhelmingly to remain a British colony.

They've grown accustomed to his face—and his cheerful welcome: "Hello, Darlin'—I love you!" Every morning, rain or shine, Johnny Barnes is at the roundabout leading into Hamilton, greeting commuters as they make their way to work. A retired bus driver, Mr. Barnes simply decided one day in 1983 that he would do his bit to bring a little joy into people's lives; a decade and a half later, he is still at it—and undoubtedly the most widely recognized and beloved person on the island.

Members of the Bermuda Regiment Band assemble in Hamilton's City Hall before a performance [facing page]. Though usually seen by the visitor in a purely ceremonial role, the Bermuda Regiment is, in its principal capacity, the island's primary external defense force.

The Regiment was formally constituted in 1965, growing out of two historic units—the Bermuda Rifles and the Bermuda Militia Artillery—which had seen service in both World Wars. Today all young Bermudian males register for military service, and the Regiment is made up of conscripts from that pool as well as volunteers, both male and female. In a scene more representative of their true purpose, a squad assaults a hill during a training exercise at Ferry Reach on St. George's Island [above].

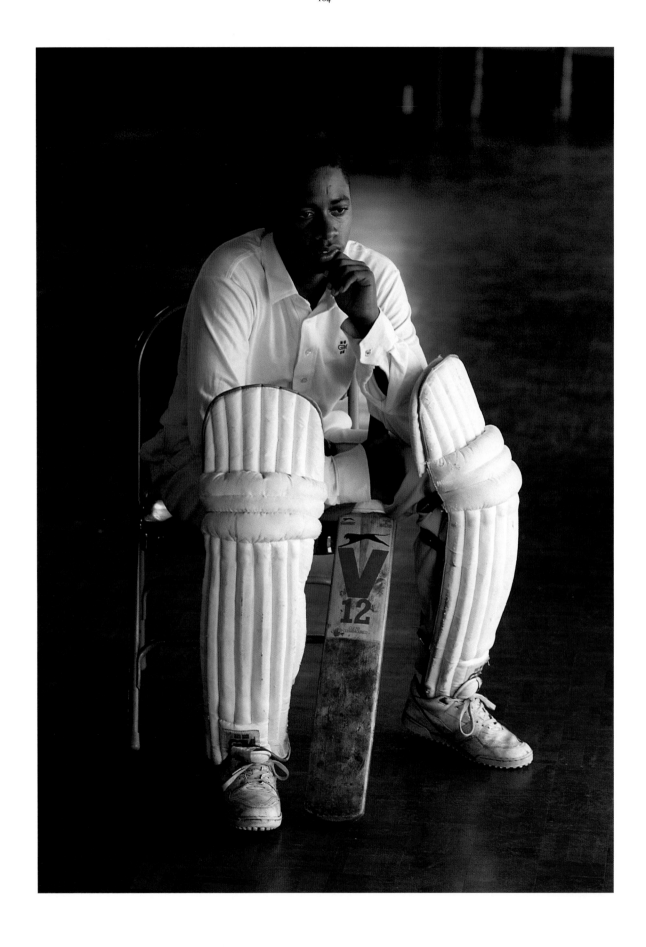

Traditional whites and decorum characterize a cricket match being played on a spring day at Lord's, the St. David's Cricket Club ground [above]. Cricket has been played on the island since the early eighteenth century, and by the mid-1800s had become a national pastime. The season finishes up with Cup Match, that annual festivity (held in commemoration of Emancipation Day, August 1, 1834) when the entire island uses cricket as an excuse to go on holiday. Perhaps dreaming of future days of glory, young cricket standout Levar Talbot watches a summer match in progress at St. George's Wellington Oval [facing page].

Cricket may have tradition on its side, but the more action-oriented sports, such as soccer [above] and rough-and-tumble rugby [facing page], seem more in tune with modern tastes. The presence of an American base on the island for a half century helped make Bermudians into ardent softball players as well, and—under the influence of cable television programming beamed in from the United States—many a Bermudian is also an impassioned fan of American football.

Bermudians' passion for the sea stretches back more than three centuries, and nowhere is that tradition more keenly felt than among the island's tiny but dedicated band of Bermuda fitted dinghy racers. Due to their cost—a dinghy with the four suits of sails needed for racing may run well over a hundred thousand dollars—and the rigors of the training schedule required to field a competitive boat, there are only a handful of active racing dinghies. [In the photograph on the facing page, the Royal Hamilton Amateur Dinghy Club's *Elizabeth* and her crew practice for a race in Hamilton Harbour.]

Lone guardian of another venerable Bermudian maritime tradition, ninety-year-old Geary Pitcher [above] still builds wooden dinghies at his boatyard on St. David's Island.

Due to its geographic isolation, Bermuda had only a scant handful of native animals, and relatively few native species of flora. Today, the overwhelming bulk of the island's vegetation has been introduced, including Bermudagrass (a native of the Mediterranean region) and virtually all of the showy flowers, such as the island's many varieties of oleander [above]. First brought to the island in the 1790s, oleander is today the floral symbol of Bermuda.

Bermuda's whistling frogs [facing page] are another human import, having been introduced from the Caribbean late in the 19th century. Though seldom seen, the tiny tree frog's piercing nighttime call guarantees that it will be heard—at least during the warmer months of the year. [Actual size of the tree frog shown: about one inch in length.]

Overlooking the south shore near Warwick Long Bay, a lone Bermuda cedar is a rare survivor of the era when the trees carpeted the island [opposite page]. The cedar played a crucial role during the first three centuries of the colony's history, providing the hard, clear wood for the island's houses and furniture, and for the swift sloops and ships which were Bermuda's economic lifeline. During and following World War II an infestation of scale insect practically obliterated the island's cedar forest, and a reforestation program began, using the casuarina, among other species.

As its name suggests, Bermudiana, shown in the photograph above, is another beloved island plant, and like the Bermuda cedar, is endemic (meaning uniquely native) to the island. A member of the iris family, Bermudiana's tiny flowers measure barely an inch across, and usually bloom during April and May.

Hamilton

Heyl's Corner, the crossroads of Hamilton, where the "birdcage" has graced the intersection of Front and Queen Streets since 1962.

The corner of Reid and Queen Streets, as seen from the Perot Post Office. While Front Street is Hamilton's showcase, Reid Street is "Main Street", where many of the capital's finest shops are found, and where Bermudians on a shopping expedition are certain to run into a friend or two.

Hamilton's Front Street faces Hamilton Harbour with a rainbow of storefronts.

During the tourist season cruise ships line Hamilton's docks and Front Street is alive with activity: taxis and carriage drivers picking up passengers, tourists trying out their new mo-peds, and package-laden shoppers crowding the storefront arcades.

Hamilton loves a celebration, and with luck, you'll see a parade, such as the one held on Bermuda Day, May 24th, when equestrians, floats, bands, majorettes, and gombeys wind their way through the capital [facing page]. On a more solemn occasion, the Bermuda Regiment Band leads a contingent of Bermuda's veterans past the Cenotaph during a ceremony commemorating the Allied victory in World War II [above].

Seat of the island's Anglican Bishopric, the Bermuda Cathedral [these pages] dominates Hamilton's skyline, and offers an unparalleled view of the city from its 140-foot tower. Consecrated in 1911, the cathedral rose from the ashes of Trinity Church, which had been destroyed by an arson fire in 1884.

The Anglican Church of Bermuda dates from 1973, when its predecessor, the Church of England, was disestablished, perhaps in recognition of the developing trend toward local autonomy in Bermudian affairs. Although it retains the largest number of adherents, and through its predecessor, claims the longest history of Bermuda's Churches, the Anglican church today coexists with more than 25 other faiths on the island.

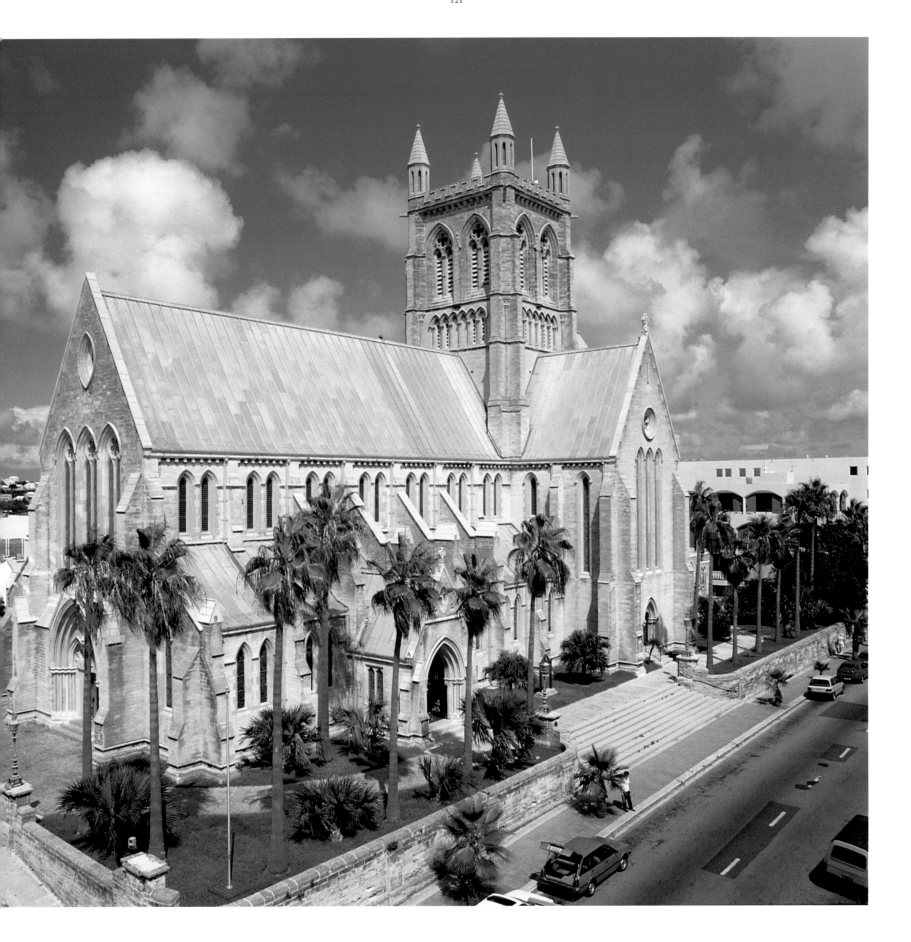

Since my earliest visit to Bermuda I have been captivated by the beauty and originality of the needle point prayer cushions which adorn the pews of the cathedral. The cushions are the work of the cathedral's Ladies' Guild, whose devoted members created some three hundred unique designs over the years, taking their inspiration from the scriptures and biblical themes [facing page].

After much coaxing, I persuaded Enith King, a longtime member of the Ladies' Guild, to allow me to photograph her working on one more cushion to add to the cathedral's collection [above].

Clad in that most famous of Bermudian creations, a pair of businessmen pause for a chat before Front Street's line of arcades. Bermuda shorts gained popularity among the islanders after Front Street clothiers created a tailored version of the shorts worn by British soldiers stationed in Bermuda. Bermuda's warm-weather "business attire", as it is commonly termed, is traditionally donned (by men only, by the way) after May 24th, the unofficial beginning of summer, although a few hardy souls wear shorts throughout the year.

Hamilton offers charming nooks, lanes, and alcoves at every turn: in a passageway linking Par-la-Ville and Bermudiana Roads, bank employee Lydia Mullin [above] takes a break and does her best to ignore a brazen neighbor trying to read over her shoulder. (The young woman in bronze is the creation of Bermuda's famed sculptor Desmond Fountain.)

Hamilton Harbour presents the city with a constantly changing panorama: cargo ships arrive throughout the year, summer brings cruise ships to line Hamilton's docks, and ferries to Paget, Warwick, and Somerset come and go throughout the day. (On the facing page, a ferry passes behind the Royal Bermuda Yacht Club, founded in 1844.)

Fall brings an annual classic to the harbour, when Bermuda hosts the Gold Cup series of races, which lures champion sailors from around the world [above].

Although from the air Hamilton appears to be a mass of commercial buildings [facing page], the city's small scale means that bucolic settings, such as this small hotel on the west side of town [above], lie only a short walk from the city center. Indeed, within its legal boundaries, Hamilton is a tiny city: a mere 177 acres, with a population of barely a thousand people by the mid-1990s. Hamilton and surrounding Pembroke Parish have been steadily losing population for half a century: after the introduction of motor vehicles in 1946, the population long concentrated around the capital began dispersing throughout the island.

Built circa 1817, the historic Sessions House [above] stands at the eastern edge of the city and is home to both the House of Assembly and the Supreme Court. (The historical record is imprecise as to the exact date of the original construction; the distinctive Italianesque towers and verandah were added in 1887, to commemorate Queen Victoria's Jubilee; the pointed spire seen between the towers is that of a church some distance behind the Sessions House.)

Hamilton's City Hall glows under a twilight sky as an audience arrives for a performance at the City Hall Theatre [facing page]. Opened in 1960, the building was the design of famed Bermudian architect Will Onions, and incorporates elements of Bermuda cottage architecture; at the top of the tower a bronze *Sea Venture* weather vane swings in the wind.

A World Apart

Pausing for a moment between fares, a Front Street hire-carriage driver evokes a scene reminiscent of a time before Bermuda knew the automobile, and horse-drawn transport was common.

A pair of show horses cavort in dawn's cool air as the sun rises over the
spire of St. Mark's Church in Smith's Parish.

When the island's agriculture was in a perilous state in the late 1800s, Portuguese farmers were recruited from the Azores, and eventually hundreds immigrated to the island. Although their descendants have since become involved in all sectors of society, it is the Portuguese, like farmworker John Barbosa, picking lettuce in a Devonshire field [facing page], who remain the stalwarts of Bermuda's farm economy. Fiercely proud of its heritage, the Portuguese community is always sure to be present on the 24th of May, when Hamilton hosts the annual Bermuda Day Parade [above].

Paget Parish is home to many of the island's grand historic houses, and on a hilltop overlooking Hamilton Harbour and the Great Sound stands Bloomfield, one of the grandest of them all [these pages]. Like many of Bermuda's great historic houses, Bloomfield evolved into its present form over a period of years, and placing a date on the original construction involves some guesswork. While the main body of the house was built between 1720 and 1800, evidence suggests that the original kitchen, now converted into a gameroom [above], may date from 1662.

One characteristic common to early Bermuda homes, large or small, is the fact that it was difficult to find cedar logs which could yield beams longer than sixteen feet, which effectively limited the width of rooms, no matter how large the house. The solution in larger homes was often to build in an "E" or "U" pattern (as with Bloomfield) which yielded a larger structure without sacrificing flow-through ventilation.

During the 18th century Bermuda developed its classic cottage architecture, using native materials: limestone for walls and roof, with cedar used for structural support, doors, windows, and interior decoration. The famous Bermuda "cake-icing" roof [shown being built, above, and in finished form on the facing page] results from the overlapping of limestone slates, covered with a sealing mortar. Once whitewashed, the roof serves as the rainwater catchment for the water tank [facing page, top right] which supplies the Bermuda home with water.

"Push-out" blinds [facing page, bottom left] shade windows from the summer sun and showers, while letting in cooling breezes, and serve as storm shutters when closed. Against all this sensible efficiency, the "eyebrow" above the push-out blinds is essentially decorative, as are the "welcoming arms" [facing page, bottom right] framing the entrance steps, which took their name from Bermuda's tradition of hospitality.

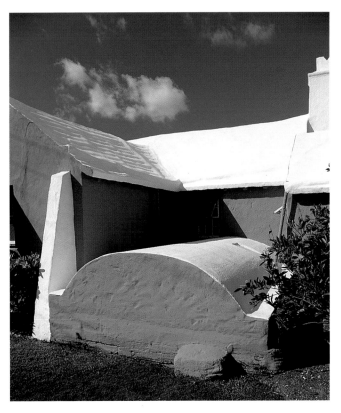

The combination of Bermuda's unique architecture and idyllic landscape has captured the imagination of world-renowned artists since the turn of the century, when Winslow Homer spent two seasons on the island, and in the past two decades it has become the favored subject of a dozen or more local professional artists as well. Working with airbrush and acrylic, Bermuda-born artist Michael Swan [above] has developed a minimalist style which brings the details of Bermuda architecture into sharp focus [facing page]. His highly realistic style—almost photographic in its impact—sets him apart from the great majority of painters of the Bermudian scene, many of whom have chosen to work in watercolors and favor a somewhat more romantic interpretation of the Bermudian landscape.

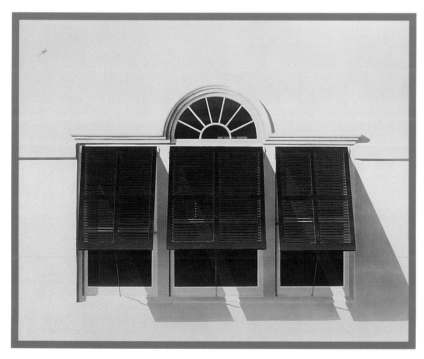

Clermont [above] has been the most regal adornment of lower Hamilton Harbour since it was built in 1800, and boasts the first tennis court ever built in the Western Hemisphere. As befits its name, nearby Overlook [facing page], built a century later, also overlooks the harbour from its location on the water side of Harbour Road.

Historically, nearly all Bermuda homes, small or large, were named, rather than numbered; not until the 1980s, in a move to improve postal deliveries, were houses systematically given numbers. Fortunately for the romantic of spirit, the names survive: some, like Mount Pleasant, Bloomfield, Norwood, Somerset, and Rosemount, to name a few, evoke poetic or historic associations, while some others—Wit's End, Sitting Pretty, Dream Come True, and Just a Start, for example—reveal a more whimsical bent. Whatever their inspiration, the names of Bermuda's houses add to the island's storied charm.

The Great Sound and Hamilton Harbour, seen from high atop Paget.

Astwood Park beach, on the south shore in Warwick Parish

An aerial view over the south shore in Southampton Parish encompasses the
Sonesta Beach Hotel, Gibbs Hill Lighthouse, and the Great Sound beyond.

Bermuda is an artist's paradise, and in the past few decades a number of locally-based painters have made names for themselves, including Alfred Birdsey (whom I featured in my first book, *Images of Bermuda*), Michael Swan (pictured earlier in this chapter), Mary Powell, Joan Forbes, Robert Bassett, and Joan Wilson. No one, however, has claimed a wider following than Carole Holding [above]. A native of England who came to Bermuda to work in the hotel industry nearly three decades ago, Miss Holding eventually returned to the passion for art she had felt in her childhood. Over the years she has developed a charming "soft" watercolor style particularly suited to her two specialties: flowers and Bermuda scenes [facing page].

The Foot of the Lane, at the eastern end of Hamilton Harbour

When I first happened upon this secluded beach late one afternoon just before sunset, it reminded me of a bygone Bermuda—Bermuda as it was before legions of tourists began their invasion of the island, and I found myself returning to it often to photograph its changing moods. Usually deserted, it is a lovely stretch of sand, a place Bermudians know well and can still call their own. With the hope that it will remain so, I have decided to leave it unidentified.

Notes

1. Sources: As will be evident from a reading of the text and captions, much of the material in this book is derived from personal observation and contact with Bermudians in the many months I have spent in Bermuda over the past sixteen years. For the historical aspects, however, I have made extensive use of the extraordinary amount of literature about the island—as of 1995, upward of eight hundred books had been published about Bermuda.

Bermudians and all lovers of Bermudian history owe a tremendous debt to Henry C. Wilkinson, author of *The Adventurers of Bermuda*, *Bermuda in the Old Empire*, and *Bermuda From Sail to Steam*. Dr. Wilkinson's three books, clearly a labor of love, are unquestionably the most thorough compilation of Bermudian history ever published, and are distinguished by a breadth of knowledge and an erudition which are as delightful to read as they are rare to encounter. Regrettably, at this writing all three titles are out of print, although they can be found in larger libraries.

Terry Tucker's *Bermuda: Today and Yesterday* provides a good overview of Bermudian history in a compact form, as does *Insight Guides Bermuda*, by Martha Zenfell (Ed.). George Rushe's *Your Bermuda* (the successor to *Bermuda, As a Matter of Fact!*) is a handy compendium of information Bermudian.

Sir John H. Lefroy's *Memorials of the Bermudas*, originally published in the 1870s, assembles an important collection of documents relating to Bermuda's early history, such as those pertaining to the island's discovery, as well as the earliest extensive accounts of the island, written by early shipwreck survivors, including May, Strachey and Jourdain.

A number of books provide a feel for the earlier decades of this century which is sometimes missing from more formal histories. Among the best are: *Bermuda Recollections* by Elizabeth Jones (Ed.); Walter Hayward's *Bermuda Past and Present*; Hudson

Strode's *The Story of Bermuda*; and Carveth Wells' *Bermuda in Three Colors*. William Zuill's classic, *Bermuda Journey*, is a captivating, often irreverent compilation of information and anecdote covering Bermuda from the founding of the colony up to the 1940s. James Smith's *Slavery in Bermuda* and Cyril Packwood's *Chained on the Rock* explore an aspect of Bermudian history which has all too often been given short shrift in other histories.

2. Picture Credits: All photographs and illustrations are by the author except as follows (page numbers indicated): 2-3: map by John Ogilby (1670); 11: Ian Murdoch; 44: detail from a map by Nicolas Sanson, "North America in 1650", original in the collection of Historic Urban Plans, Ithaca, New York; 46-47: original painting by Richard W. DeRosset, ASMA, © Imágenes Press; 51: painting by Christopher Grimes, original in the collection of the Bank of Bermuda, Hamilton; 52-53: aquatint by Captain Brown, (Joseph Stadler, engraver) (1816), from an original in the National Maritime Museum, Greenwich, London; 55: The Granger Collection, New York; 56-57: original painting by Richard W. DeRosset, ASMA, © Imágenes Press; 61: painting by Thomas Driver (1823), courtesy Bermuda Archives; 67: aquatint by Captain Brown, (Joseph Stadler, engraver) (1816), from an original in the Mayor's Parlour, Hamilton City Hall, courtesy the Corporation of Hamilton; 70-71: original painting by Richard W. DeRosset, ASMA, © Imágenes Press; 75, 76, 78: courtesy Bermuda Archives; 79: courtesy Bermuda Department of Tourism; 83: Emory Kristof/National Geographic Image Collection; 106, 107: Lawrence Trott; 141: paintings by and courtesy of Michael Swan; 149: paintings by and courtesy of Carole Holding.

Limited-edition lithographs of the Richard De Rosset paintings are available from the publisher.

Acknowledgements

Bermudians are an exceedingly generous and open people, and this book owes a great deal to that national personality; more times than I can remember, people have given me, often as a total stranger, access to their homes, property, records, and time to facilitate my photography or research. Beyond these casual and often fleeting encounters, I am deeply indebted to the following—a number of whom I am privileged to call my friends—for the information, background, guidance, assistance, and hospitality they extended over the months I spent preparing this book: George and Claire Rushe, Kathie Gosling, Kay Gosling, Teddy Gosling, John and Alice Eggmann, Bob and Helen Hay, Robert and Lisa Rosser, Mr and Mrs Conrad Engelhardt, Brian Benevides, Jerome Levine, Manuel Lopes, John Barbosa, Vivienne Gardner, Anne Powell, Hubert Watlington, Gillian White, Michael Cherry, Mike Smatt, Stephen Gale, Horst Augustinovic, Richard and Bobbie Gorham, Fanshaw Lamb, Michele Smith, Joan Forbes, Bruce Sims, Sheldon Johnstone, Judy Michie; Claire Spencer and St. Peter's Church; Helena Rawlings and the Bermuda Cathedral; Rosa Hollis, Bermuda Railway Museum; Bermuda National Trust; Heydon Trust; Somers Cooper, John Musson, George Robinson, and the Royal Bermuda Yacht Club; Royal Hamilton Amateur Dinghy Club; Gary Phillips and Charles Webbe, Bermuda Department of Tourism; John Adams, Sandra Rouja, and Karla Hayward, Bermuda Archives; Clevelyn Crichlow and Phyliss Basden, Bermuda Post Office; Roger Sherratt and the Corporation of Hamilton; Loretta Kyme Thompson and the Bank of Bermuda; the Bank of Butterfield; Eldon Trimingham, Gail Stuart, Kenneth Simons, and Trimingham's; Captain Kenny Todd and crew of *Faithful*; Captain Peter Simons and crew of *Powerful*; Pilot Warden Keith Battersbee and crew of *St. David's*; Capt. Henry Simpson, Capt. Dill, Lt. David Curley, and the Bermuda Regiment; ACE Insurance, OIL Insurance, Strategic Asset Management, Mid-Ocean Reinsurance; Maria and Donald MacPherson, John S. Darrell Co.; Ocean View Farm; Mid-Ocean Club; Bermuda Photo Craftsmen; Bermuda Helicopters; West Point Museum; The Boeing Company; Chris Small, Lamont-Doherty Earth Observatory, Columbia University; Daniel Nguyen, Modern Graphics; and to Tim Sweeney, Ella LaBrucherie, and Martha Hoch for assistance with the editorial process.

Published in the United States of America by
Imágenes Press
Post Office Box 1150
Pine Valley, California 91962 USA
Tel: (619) 473-8676   Fax: (619) 473-8272
Tel: (935) 473-8676   Fax: (935) 473-8272
Email: ImagenesPress@aol.com

Design Consultant: Geneva Design Studio
Printed in China

Bermuda, A World Apart
ISBN 0-939302-32-2 (Standard Edition)

Bermuda

(Scale: 1 inch = 1.3 miles / 1 cm. = 0.82 km.)

IRELAND ISLAND N.

Royal Naval Dockyard & B. Maritime Museum

Grassy Bay

Somerset Long Bay

Mangrove Bay

Daniel's Head

IRELAND ISLAND S.

BOAZ I.

Somerset Village

WATFORD I.

Sandys

SOMERSET ISLAND

Dundonald Channel

Spanish Pt.

Deep Bay

MAIN ISLAND

Fort Scaur

Great Sound

Ely's Harbour

Somerset Bridge

Two Rock Passage

Point Shares

Pembroke

Hamilton

Port Hamilton

Devonshire

Hawkins I.

Long I.

Ports I.

Hamilton Harbour

Spring Benny's Bay

Grace I.

Darrell's I.

Spithead

Hinson's I.

Botanical Gardens

Devonshire Bay

Whitney Bay

Little Sound

Burgess Point

Hungry Bay

Grape Bay

West Whale Bay

Southampton

Warwick Pond

Warwick

Paget

Elbow Beach

Coral Beach

Warwick Camp

Church Bay

Gibb's Hill Lighthouse

Christian Bay

Boat Bay

Sinky Bay

East Whale Bay

Horseshoe Bay

Chaplin Bay

Warwick Long Bay

Marley Beach

Astwood Park

Wha. Bone

Coney

Bailey's Bay

The Crawl

Hamilton

Shelly Bay

Lea.

Trunk I.

Harringto. Sound

Flatts Inlet

Aquarium, Museum & Zoo

Flatts

Smith's

Spittal Pond

Spanish Rock

Atlantic Ocean

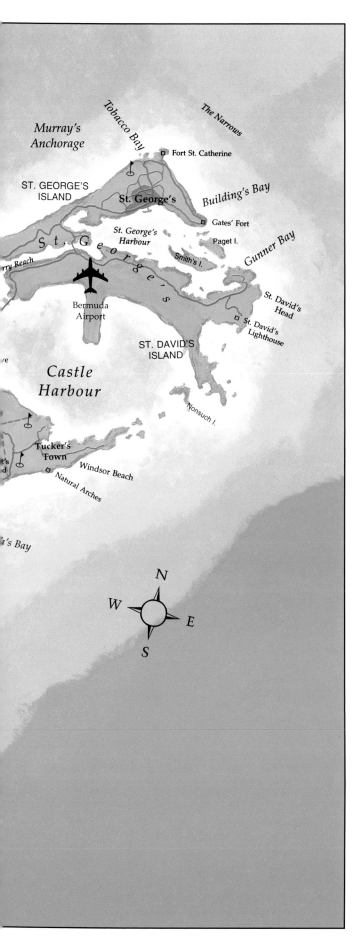

Location and geography: Bermuda is an island group composed of more than 130 islands (the number of islands depends on how small a rock outcropping is counted as an island) with a total land area of approximately 21.6 square miles (55.6 square kilometers), located in the western North Atlantic Ocean (32° 18' N., 64° 45' W.) 649 statute miles (1043 kilometers) east of Cape Hatteras, North Carolina, the nearest point of continental land. Bermuda is the exposed tip of an extinct volcano, capped by a layer of aeolian limestone of a generally hilly aspect (maximum elevation, at Town Hill, Smith's Parish: 259' (79 meters).

Population: 58,000 (1996 est.); virtually all of the population resides on the seven principal islands joined by bridges. Bermuda's population density of about 2760 people per square mile is very high compared to other countries. (Although it of course pales by comparison with selected urban areas, such as Manhattan Island, which is approximately the same size as Bermuda.)

Government: British colony, internally self-governing under a written constitution. A Governor appointed by the British Crown has nominal authority over foreign relations and security matters. Bermuda's Parliament, elected by universal adult suffrage, dates from 1620, and is the oldest of the British Commonwealth parliaments outside the British Isles.

Economy: Based principally on international business (insurance, reinsurance, financial services, international corporate headquarters, and "exempt" companies), with tourism as the second-largest foreign-exchange earner.

Climate: Mild, humid, sub-tropical, moderated by prevailing southwesterly winds and the Gulf Stream; rainfall is distributed fairly evenly throughout the year; daytime temperature in the warm season (April-November) is in the mid-70s to mid-80s° F. (mid-to-high 20s° C.), and in the mid-60s° F. (about 16-18° C.) in the cool months (December-March).

Miscellaneous: Language: English. **Religion:** predominantly Protestant, significant minority of Roman Catholic adherents; complete freedom of religion. **Motto:** *Quo Fata Ferunt* (wherever the fates may lead us).

The sun sets over Ely's Harbour in Sandys Parish